Securities AI

Programs Conceptual

Investigative – Sanctuary – Communications

Julien Coallier

Note from Author

This overall text is a securities grand system AI design meant for securities: centering on investigative, setting a parameter (sanctuary) and establishing communications (data-centre). As grand system, you as reader and entrepreneur, innovator, can reform applicable content per mention, to establish an initial systems long term design, adding features as technology or resource enable.

Overall, the grand systems formation is intended for a networks of securities usage, where the mandate information derived is used as a resource to control or management asset coordination or protected environments. Within an overall mapping of the structured system, you answer all the questions (selected), of which filled in, the AI as automated intelligence, has the answers to perform with. As performance driven, the results and management usage are displayed, as a control room. Enabling as communications, a central display used for organization.

Contents are a conceptual framework focusing on investigative, setting a parameter (sanctuary) and establishing communications (data-centre), each intended filled-in/created separate, and overall united into a framework design.

Investigative: Judiciary Core

Investigation Commission

- Commission as organized executive requirement in protection. Defence of title

    - Report building in determination of fact finding

        - Premise of investigation defined/identified (assassination, invasion, and corruption thereby afflicting operational executive power structure within supreme structures

- Hearing as meeting to identify premise concerns

    - Identifying meaning correlates with face value, proposed intentions, and overall resulting force/intervention/notice (such as severe alarm)

* An extensions of satisfying oaths and affirmations

    - A protective entitlement granted within taking oaths and affirmations

Commission Office-Organization as Embodiment

    - Archives witness accounts

    - Receive, catalog, verify scientifically if applicable, and secure evidence

    - Create records of participation whose formality of entry is itself verified, explained, introduced

    - Safekeeping a record of staff, work, progress, and concluded reports and other relevant paperwork categorized as secondary per report as reference material

    - Formal liaisons during operations as field or operational reports

Paperwork as

(Assumed integrated into live record keeping, automated categorization, reference building)

*Judicial as core, as intelligence core embedded

- Signatures to operate executive orders (signature, seal, permissions granted by default levels within supreme structure)

- Evaluation criteria

    - Premise per evidence findings/location-driven

    - Maps, visual aids, onsite virtual environment (virtual snapshots)

    - Professional findings per function/specialization

    - Occupation, status within supreme structure (such as education) of witness

- Relevancy to investigation (location, timing, sensory, speculative as frequency of occurrence and in relation to locations, timing, sensory)
    - Resolutions passed since investigation began, and implications such as if impeding, deliverance, counter formations notice

- Requests from upper powers for information during investigation, concerning collected information

    - Data trap to measure frequency of interest in speculative assertion/addition

        - Counting access, breaches

- Power-structure interpretations to oath stipulations

    - Personal communications

    - Requests to use privilege

- Formal witness statements as stated

    - Transcript

    - Recording

    - Visual media

- Visual exhibition

- Log of editing, sign off on edits

- Prepared for printing services

- Prepared per level of authoritative request

*Highlighting/categorization of data flooding (color coding information based on relevancy, including therein for faint and brief important information within largescale information (assumed called burying)

- Cycling overall contents collected in investigation against large volume bulks added into as volumes (such as prefabricated, so called archived)

Questioning

- Establishing state of mind within scenario, context stated

Witness account - Purpose of Hearing Participation

- Establishing how each interview relates to investigation, including strategically within a mapped context, or scenario

    - Explaining evidence in relation to validating the context or scenario mapped

*Assurance the witness is of sound state of mind, participating according to regulatory safeguards (explaining rights, operational standard)

    - Providing automated information panel

* Readying a media ready, recap, or evaluation of hearing

Participant Options Selection
- Refreshments
- Housing
- Information references (schedules, conduct expectations, attire)
- Interpreter assigned

Daily Occupation - Mapping Status, Progression

*Inconsistencies as one presented as the other

    - Relationships - Primary as pattern (contextual long term)

        - Friends

        - Romantic

        - Hired, Contractual

- Primary:	Interactions	**Secondary:**	Moment to moment (contextual short term Interaction)
- Primary:	Work details	**Secondary:**	Leisure
- Primary:	Travel	**Secondary:**	Exploration

*Ease of occupation (onsite easement, difficulties: conflicts and solutions)

Mapping Daily Occupation

(Establishing overall timeline)

*Ease vs Difficulty

*Standard definition vs. acknowledged meaning

*Plans vs. alterations met

    - Corresponding evidences

*Durations

*Locations

*Type of communication (used in correlation to mapped occupation)

    - Non coherent

    - Brief, informative in-the-passing

    - Continued discussion

    - Professional courtesy

    - Assessments made onsite

        - Comments, suggestions detailing meaning

            - Constrictions pointed out?

            - Measurements

            - Mentions of future planning due to there as contextual remedy

            - Is the comment out of the ordinary for that person yet contextually appropriate?

*Accessibility

*Privilege status and timeline if applicable

Mapping Validity of Evidence

- Evidence corresponding soundly to claims

- Evidence not corresponding to claims

Mapping Evidence History

- Known whereabouts of evidence

- Known interactions with evidence

- Symbolic meanings of evidence as stated

- Identifying rarity of evidence if a factor

- Alterations to evidence?

Establishing Frame of Mind

- References sought

- Specialized knowledge

- Biological factors (contentious, influencing or sensibilities altering)
    - Hunger, pain, physical discomfort; sensory
    - Euphoric, substances

- Gender bias, does the gender admit bias, is there a biological conditioning involved for abnormalities

- Relevancy to abstract mentions for specific questions
    - Noting abstractions responded, for potential evaluation later (such as towards a

        Seemingly unrelated yet relevant mention)

- National interests

Establishing Extent of Knowledge

- Determining something is good

- Determining something isn't bad

- Determining something is bad

- Determining without making judgements whether things are good or bad

- Determining authoritative involvement, interference

- Doctrines or references being adhered to, timeline for the progress of interpreting/using knowledge

*Does evidence suggest formal status contradicts determination of knowledge?

*Are there factors preventing, so called easing or otherwise infringing determination (embedded in the social configuration, agency interfering/involved

*Authoritative passes received, in relation to registered involvement

    - Are registered involvements beings interfered/intervened against?

        - Data trap allocations to test for spies (baiting registry conspiracies)

*Publically stated sympathies, public as in commercial or industrial spaces with strangers and acquaintances

*Any defamation or slander publically broadcasted, or privately if orchestrated among stranger and acquaintances towards person being investigated (strategic formation to harm another)

    - Any mention of authorities qualification/backing

    - Examining local powers possible approached, paperwork exchanged if applicable

    - If found, is the agency of the individual or group paid for, on salaries to defame, slander

        - baiting for misuse of technologies, for attempts to covertly manage local population into mob vendettas

        - Schemes found to harass, intimidate,

        - Determining broader conspiracies of invasive agency if applicable

Describing Conversations

- Level of accuracy in remembering

    - What forms of opinion are involved?

- Forms of approval mentioned, implied as sensory or contextual of counterintuitive (deliberately difficult to assess?)

- Gifts, substances, pleasure orientated gratifications as contextual

- Changes in attitudes, timelines and to individuals, groups, or everybody

- Changes in noticing, timelines and to individuals, groups, or everybody

- Was there a translation, interpretation factor?

    - Was it correct?

Conversations Classification

- Structural powers (formal administrative)

- Applications (general technological)

- Print as memos, notes, and letters

Conversation Highlights

*Strategic implication

Protest

Requests

Reviewing past interview highlights

- On site - Potential note to examine past interviewers, or company to interview

- On site - Potential re-examination of previous premises, commission orders, formal budget of all teams assigned for investigation, along timeline, review access,

- On Site calculation reference checker of distances stated, travel undertaken vs. possible travel confirmed, adding additional regional emergency modified timetables

Tactical Considerations

As generally based on biologically driven sensory narrative

(Body reacts from previous conditioning vs. on site appearance)

*Places into question training, conditioning, or lack thereof

- Relief or happiness

- Gain or reflection of overall new requirements

- Excitement or favorably pleasing

- Excuse/excused confusion or surprised response

- Heard rumor that seemed relevant to the acknowledgement, or formal questioning of circumstance of actual situation

- Is an opposing outburst joining overall esteems of meaning as exemplified (delayed peer pressure response or adherence towards a location/precedence)

(Imitation, or actually an unusual outburst?)

- Unusual for that person, or for that location

- Is the person being interrupted, such meal time privilege/ritual interrupted

- Being rewarded or being gifted

- Survived situation or completed objective

- Automated response to symbolic value, or part of an overall criminal conspiracy

Becoming too speculative

Start referring back to stronger point of interest, or restate premise

- Previous comments mentioning having issues, yet investigator mapping where, if or where the person is affecting others differently

- Was the person trained to train others?

- Personal behaviour notes becoming too irrelevant, tabloid notes warning

- Hiding in tabloid like atmosphere?

*Examining grounds for planted evidence, speculative leads intuition

*Re-examination of evidence of a specific location, from a specific source or sources

(Circulate through authoritative requests, civics data)

  - Planted evidence to invalidate potential witness

  - Planted evidence as political favor

  - Planted evidence as corrupted attempt for quick promotion

  - Planted evidence to start larger conflict

*Data trap, quick and easy evidence planting area

*Allowance to ask varying information as logged and subject to not gaining towards media as on duty performance only

  - Checking for gifts, benefits granted towards questioning red flagged

*Ability for those investigated to red flag interview standards, conditions

  - Automated red flags as, investigation receiving non monitored communications asking to mistreat

  - Allowing for resting quarters for investigators preventing red flags or to relax interviewee threatening to red flag

  - Allowance for refreshment snack, such as water, bread relevant to race (wheat, rice, vegan), and with protein as meal for prolonged

- Allowance for questioning under substances selected, recorded

  * Assumes corruption/spies will disrupt to intimidate or reduce valuable details and recommend further disruptive intervention as if social benefit

Interviewing to create a Character Profile

(Understandably misleading, belligerent as)

- Traumatic experiences, or extreme actions assumed relevant to traumatic instances

- Common themes, subjects talked about

- Nationalistic opinions (timeline assessment as required if valid-proof is brought up of living in occupied/corrupted state)

> - Race context as, if you're not the leader's race your opinions if considered valid are thereby all racist?

> - Is there reason to believe both agreeing and disagreeing subjects interviewee as wrong, bad, mean?

- Relevant to peer pressures

- Devoid of community support, when worst and or actual offenders are supported

Interviewing to create a Character Profile - Activities

- Registered status of group if applicable

- Plans made based on paperwork

- Main people interacted with in relation to activities shared

*Requirements for activities/membership

* Rituals of appreciation involved

** System safeguard against repeated questioning where systematic (Corrupted authorities) abuse is mentioned, and overall contradict questioning, yet subject or approach is continually entertained

> - Such as authorities used to disrupt, harm were noticed yet now the investigation is trying to use results as evidence without explaining their involvement

** System safeguard against fake profiles found across various locations

Contextual Implications - Focusing on Investigation Commission Premise

- Whereabouts relevance of events causing an investigation commission

    - Are there differences in authoritative procedure in that location (who controls autopsies, quarantine, surveillance, emergency services?)

    - Who has priority to escort, whom was filled into play/operations\?

    - Examining censorship over reporters

    - Searching for trophy symbols, such as at the cometary embedded into design

    - Trophy recordings kept based on pained voices, misery, suffering, such as within investigative or other authoritative archives

Fake Contextual Implications - Indicative of not focusing on Investigation Commission Premise until, because of structural blockades

*Potential context for corruption and conspiracy to intertwine, or are intertwined

    - Obvious support rewards to undermine those interviewed, causing a need to approach unacceptable contacts out of desperation/withdrawal

    - Examination of stated presumption vs budgets assumed self-allocated

    - Overall declarations against standard operations by authoritative voices

        - Are there solutions recommendations, or just blanket criticism?

    - Do some of the testimony areas keep being resented, distorted, or otherwise retried endlessly

    - Inability to be impressed, such as from emerging breakthroughs, clarifications

    - Changes to authoritative powers, emergency services, before or near the offence being investigated

        - Do they offer fabricated view of what happened?

        - Are they invalidating service ability?

        - Are there long term punitive decisions made to internal service?

        - Does their blood match their last name?

            - Rounding up of invalid name as spy cleanse

    - Are harmful speculations being collected and then forwarded to media to become common knowledge?

        - Relates to corruption trying to maintain or increase budgets of a non-relevancy though possibly very tabloid/rumor-gossip perspective

Quality Assurance - Agency (Assigned) Specific

- Easement of secured contact, information submission vis-a-vis questions asked

- Phone app from governmental site able to verify an agent's badge, or ID with voice, and or appearance

- Scheduled visitation as crypto secured ID verification (one way only)

- Limited duration, does not verify on a later or other than scheduled date/duration

- Assumes crypto is able to process paperwork, ID

- Intended to be held in a secured, no public entry Acari center

- Easement for interviewed to submit stories for approval, bound for media release

- Assumed allowed after investigation is over, possible fee attached with forwarding to select medias

- Having to color highlight which areas of the pieces come from different authors or sources

- Long term semi-passive monitoring of high profile, knowing relevant outsiders likely to try communicating

- Defence packages as privilege to drink, substances at specific locations monitored

- Relocation packages as in light/formal-support of talents or willingness for isolation without the extra pay, yet benefits of security semi-on call

- Identifying photos to (assume multiple people (4 as witness tendency expected) used to identify

- Names

- Voice samples

- Locations

- Time periods/dates

- Security clearance info (premise, limitations of power thereof) for photos

*If photos unclear or as secondary requirement as high profile, segmented inner investigation, with identifying with sound or names as central

- Tone of responses within timeline, such as to indicate ongoing abuse of visitation

- Correlation of behaviour modification per interactions of a particular source (narrowing interests from speculation)

- Budget examination, assessment, of either authority or individual arriving stealth: such as organized or lone mission as-organized crime (yet indications of being a group)

- Duration of any investigation or mention of lone mission as indicating fake profiles, such as across a network of corruption (*name/registry conspiracies)

- Request that witness not mention personal remarks, and notifying that during scheduled (formal) interview remarks given can, will be discussed about

Universal Clarification Request

(Is there a pattern of abuse resembling romantic entanglement, preventing criminal intentions, breaking personal requests?)

Request to remove sympathetic/unsympathetic comments, or clarification as:

Are titled or authoritative voices being used to create sympathy vouches, indicative of conspiracy/manipulation by mentionable?

- Use of faith figures that whose preaching may be valid, and admitting attendance

    *Vs. Spending time and effort convincing a relationship is fake, flawed, ruined

- Use of consoling having witnessed investments of emotional outcry

    * Vs. Seeking another location, relationship, establishing paperwork

- General emotional appeal by anyone deemed special interest

    * Vs. Having reasons from a perspective required to be firm, stable, coherent

- Autoreactive reassessments, resentments against authority

    * Vs. being in trouble for not siding with popular resentments

* Removed or reduced on the principal of, you can follow anyone of these people to a toilet and have them stink, or keep them up for long enough and have them raving mad: *Context not being applied.

- Assumes proving mental illness by the insane standards of procedure results in requests to abuse power, yet can involve perfectly typed, and sounding reports

Universal Recommended Behaviour

For investigator and asset building/proof-finding principal for those interviewed

- Remaining refreshed for conducting detailed questioning/answering

- Creating temporary housing options for high asset monitoring

> * No privacy clauses assumed required signed into, with an automated censorship of toiletry sounds

> * Baiting allowances, for interviewed to target fake profile originators into verbal confession for reward

> * Death traps in association to easy entry for fake surveillance to enter and die

> *Creating off limits signage as required standard to ward off trespassing

- Assumption that anyone who has had anything has done it or is good at it, as subject to not being remembered

(As likely after traumatic questioning into speculative conjuncture)

Detailing Atmosphere

Products of Environment Analysis/Indicator

(A notice of how the individual interpreted interactions custom to their arrangement)

- Common symbolic attributes worn, outspoken at specific locations or in general regions

- Type of culture perceived at locations

- Level of sophistication found at an area

- Level of discipline commonly displayed

- Names of reference in the general locations

- Approximation of vital to person services, in connection to other services also generally associated or required

- Is the area reserved for stealth operations, mobilized for specialized purposes?

> - Training grounds nearby?

- Any means of enabling stealth movements

- Specialized equipment in the area required in relevancy to premise of investigation?

Paid Revisits

Capitalism Meets Popular Interest

If key words have been exhausted, and a data trap is set simply to reveal popularity, so that paid interview or portions earned forwarded as percentage of gain contracted to interview an exhausted investigation, for details meant for movie, news, and media related clarity

- As options appearing in investigation segment of accessible by applications to those interviewed

- Assumes crypt securement for payments

- Assumes after investigation is over, yet popularity is causing clarity to be in good nature of depicting nevertheless a tragic event

    - Likely requires time after mourning, after rebuilding, after restoring as applicable etc..

*Ongoing mail of support as indicator

*Opening of access to judge, authorities, witnesses for media related references, possibly collected during trial during off time logged, at home, own equipment, as into personal preapproved data vault associated to case

    - Potential bibliographical or museum works as options checked into by case, by year

    - Potential clearance requirements as paid to be forwarded (assumed media production)

Censored Materials for Media Conversion

- Injury depictions as graphic colored displays, enough for movie effect modeling only

- Removal of nudity from crime scene, or investigative exploration

- Invasion of privacy as disqualifier to material usable

Highlighting Special Persons, Agency Talents

Possibly unprofessional, conspiracy like atmosphere detectable, as fine and relevant per expertise, yet the investigation requires clear and concise

- Persons qualified across multiple jurisdictions, or across structures of power

- Elevated esteems participating (especially assigned, under what premise?)

- Witnesses giving detailed historic context

*Issue in adding too much information into speculative interest

*Issue in attempts as stealth movement involved with evidence

*Like finding a high volume of people arriving to explain a person has not value or importance, such as multiple times towards everyone in a given population (Budget access thereby applicable, what incentive? Whose design?). Flamboyant usage of specialist?

President's Remarks / President's Panel (Information Access)

- Notes on creation of commission

    - Brief notes added as reference, such as contextual, historical record building

        - Add on (formal approvals, explanations) of subsequent compartmentalized investigations within scope of premise

        - Office to office, originating commission office as holder-of-controls of all viewable data

        - Assumed held into, stored in Acari holdings, as thereby backup and storage held (digitally, in hardware) overnights

- Involved primarily with federal, international intelligence as applicable, and departments of state security (levels of access assumed per regional representation)

        - Settings based on filled in criteria for viewing, formalities like premise, oaths universally viewable

Specialist Panel

(As delivering insight (not in investigation, such as special invite, appearance)

- Creating narratives, such as useful for political script writers

- Explaining detailed conclusions

- Providing system relevancy conclusions such as to upgrade, facilitate in relevancy of highlighted materials

Counsel Premise Indicators/Criteria for Specialist Panel

- Direction set by members of appointed commission, under premise of executive powers initiating investigation commission

    - General Counsel as referenced opinion exemplified, expertise expected

        - Assisting directors, managers across pivotal system junctures

        (Institution leaders, lead within operations)

            - General staff/enforcement input, breakthroughs, reports

            - Qualifying witnesses

            - Evidence summaries

            - Services used (assumed federal, regional clearance)

- Objective as pro state, pro glorification in terms of title secured, nation promoted

    - Creation, highlighting of memorial sites

    - Highlighting patriotic love notes, yet not actually in the formalities of the commission premise, as meaning not to be a basis of argument investigating

        - Potential brawl allocations as reasonable, semi permissible as volunteer work as potential punishment, or extra overtime hours

            - Volunteer work can (as part of, yet not the sum total) be cleanup, apologies, and empty promises of sobriety

Explanations Designed in Form:

(Template as formatted towards academically acclaimed guidelines mentioned)

*Some of these as folder content or grouped folder content, enabling other folders to be completed, and vice versa.

*Cross analysis available of form/content-structure itself

- Story form

- Fact finding form

- Timeline form

- Visual mapping

- Specialists viewpoint

- Historical, record book

- Evidence summery

    - Identification standards used/accepted

        - System upgrade panel, to upgrade authoritative safekeeping and lab-analysist (facilitation)

        - Accepted secured transportation, collections

- Testimonial if different than other forms

- Witness account if different than other forms

- Comical as likely notes form, vague references

- General Principal as guidance edicts, emergency guidance, delicate and otherwise difficult orientations to update public

    - Emergency broadcast material
- Speculation / quarantined

- Propaganda

    - Themed

- Capital assets and descriptions

- Travel timelines

Sanctuary

Note from Author

This text has been formulated using I Ching, and converted into a sanctuary command mandate

Mandate Template

This doctrine expects/assumes the surrounding environment can be studied, monitored, by an infrastructure able to defend workers, such as in the prediction, verification and notification, all as default vital expression

Creating a hierarches of performance filters, modifiers

The sage as meaning in knowing how to function, and holding premise in regards to direction as an ideal, including formalities of subject matter and purpose

- Experiment as in development from, by a state/stage of completeness in paperwork

- Of a book/doctrine/program bound: complete

Of House-program, Traditions Formal: Sanctuary

Main Program: Settings Formality in Command

*Media technologies as granted linked source to collective vote in filters

Traditions Template, of which command is usable as per regional in affirmation of compatibility along written premise.

- Per communication as standard (Access privilege: ID allocations)

- Automated posting of proficient usage (Records of ID usage, Id status)

- For traditions/domestic technological leadership (controlled by owner as command structure)

- Emplacements for the safety of occupancy, along walled structured, roofed in comfort, the light, as well as promoting intelligible faith rendering

Transitioning Core
Comparing backup to active for alterations non-conforming)

Examining if general formal failure in one screen, room, building, region, would still be passed, and even valued within another specialized avenue of direction/lifestyle co-habitation

Reminding that decent positioning, thereby focuses on highlighted areas of service potential required

- Background of streaming rivers, artistic water and light fixtures as constant change, fixed change as bound to shapes, progression highlighted as exceeding shape of view

Training Grounds
Testing

- Use of senses (applying securities viewing to sensory input)

- Notes of influence (inner development considerations, needs, future devices suggested)

- In relevancy to the supreme powers

    (As education, politics as panel, justice, military, faith, media, civics network approved)

*Mutual satisfaction, a default equities in measure, In consideration of contractual influence of criteria, requirements in relation to securities.

Ordering others based on:

- Being able to order due to having a command (Requires cores arrangements of judgement-core)

- Augmenting the satisfaction of clause/agreement (altering quality standards, within defaults established a integrity verified, as alterable)

- Testament to freedom and good will, in terms of God and manifest destiny in nature of doctrine per esteem in hope mentionable. (Intended graceful, expects misuse of symbolic, authoritative permissions to try and hack bypass, such as in preparation to counter emergencies and settings)

    o   Parades

    o   Festive celebrations

- Navigating into family planning in regards to delicate scheduling, and or access, privileges attached. Formal mapping, lock into benefit packages, such as move to communal as similar occupation.

    - Established regulatory priorities or default command/overriding moment to moment as part of family packages. Potential buy in, exchange and transfer, as meaning shifts in social parameters

Indication of command

- Mutual affirmation of ID

- Options to direct/shift trajectory

- Status display of successful ad in progress

- Scheduling of assets, services, production

Indication of Health

- Firmness in relation to proposed default form (as per individual basis, yet systems known)

    - If given a place to live, is not invaded upon, such as by

    - Trained professionals (as varied)

    - Large crowds (as inciting majority rule, and or at victim/minority grievance)

    - Extortion as draining with no refill, refresh, nor indication of usefulness

    - Stature as having become in esteems with connectivity to worth, as production enabling resources (management as administrative), assumed such as for the fabrication towards long life and other options of continuity

The significance of required

- Criteria with long term requirements as both priority and set aside during maturing processes

- Creating scheduling, such as to require timed criteria/service

    - Holding records of methods as legacy approach/enabled

- To advantage those proficient in working, as expression of any vigor besides tone, action, conceptual overall.

- Training of expression, such as using simulation

Establishing Settings Database

Settings - Character mapped as tendencies

Resources relevant to display information: Vital to know, to look for

- Action highlights (contextual as when, where, who, why, what)

- Placement in relation to supreme structural powers

  - Access/Privilege listing

  - Disruptive or symbolic titles filter/safeguard

- Favored cultural works

- Travel packages

- Titles

- Submissions (docile)

- Difficulty ratings, criteria, training grades

- Person's whereabouts vis-à-vis their scheduled performance/events

  - Access and privilege calculations based on

    - Supportive members

    - Voted upon solutions

    - Crypto projects

- Parental settings

- Feedback

Settings – Vitals-Control /Emergencies Support

- Expression/monitoring of large movements

- Status of ongoing missions/announcements/statements

- Announcement floats over current imagery if no scheduling correction has been made, until end of broadcasts, as cycled

*Ability to bypass member operations and notify in specific limited area, due to settings

Exhibition

Exhibition – Media/Artifacts

- Schedule of in house inventory, galleries, workshops

- Inventory manifest

- Selection of exhibition options possible

*An appeal to sympathy as filter

Guide-Aid

Development

- Options to engage communications/media tools in defensive manner

- To increase fortune, such as through specialized searches?

- Set towards specific correcting influences, such as language learning

- National policies information, adherence per memberships assumed

- Dating programs, family packages to encourage union forging

   - Assumes state can, wants to enable function-performance based bloodline mergers

   - Encouraging large scale cohabitation projects/networked access/privileges structured

Determination of Actions
- In appreciation to regions of custom conditioning set forth as faith indoctrination

- Bound by integrity as bypass adherence

*Desires signed into

- Pleasures under premise (sexual service standards)

- Enjoyment/appreciation standards for relationships

- Inclusion, exclusion of romance

*Potential interventions, notified

- Marriage privileges (determination of access, empowerment of participant)

- Potential rewards/penalty assignment per breach

*Cultural understanding the young sister if mature, tends to be sought after first

- Exclusion of sibling in overall cohabitation arrangements including combined romance, romance as packages

- Breeding programs as requiring sibling wanting to breed together much all have resources to own living habitation, extending lesbian right to breeding quality of life right

- Prevents men/women form reserving all females in a location to disfavor able towards each woman (assumes attachment to sexual dedication as industry, personal organization standard allowed, enforceable).

*Assumes the man/women will use all resources to seduce, then segment resources causing initial entry to be false, non-coherent/relevant to appreciation of courting purposes: determination of earnest

- Prevents men/women from conducting in appropriate acts meant to disrupt, disgrace condoning of women as to make them unattainable towards initial image of entry proposed as acceptable until, such as intoxication, slight privilege into sever control of access

- The use of wisdoms as in formalities the premises required upkeep as standard of marriage or breeding sought into, contracted onto the basis of (determinations standing)

- Considers bloodwork to be usable to identify defaults of man or woman and attachment of modified: man, woman, man modified, woman modified.

Reserved Right

- All actions committed against these are actions considered evil, as meaning no trespassing, no invitation, as meaning conditions required to upkeep access privilege (likely)

- Maturity basis as meaning, it is understood early entry is a means to condition simplicity of acceptance without merit on, in intellectual means (non-exemplar form)

- In protection of male, void of false networked readied of inappropriate female, inappropriate from female such as to bypass non exclusion formally states required

- Reversal of double reserved rights into mutual inclusion accord, leeway as falling in love of geniuses, bodily geniuses, or technological merger into wonderment (assumed appropriate, possible)

    o Intelligence and movement of above ability, grade, as natural bypass to boundaries, significance of causing a need to claim reserved right on basis of performance

    *Subject to what criteria of inclusion (Nullifier of reserved rights?)

    *Becomes a matter of abandonment except towards reincarnation as privilege for elimination of those dangerous as against non-contact yet with addition of reincarnation readied

    (Meaning not having relationship yet adding death traps in protection of placing formalities towards reincarnation approvals simply)

    *Potential automated system usage to couple offspring from both would be romance, after several generations away from initiating parents whom reproduced elsewhere, removable without penalty.

    - As meaning overnight romance/encounters as potential initiation across bloodiness, to statistically declare overall probability of success towards emerging new generations uncertain of coupling potential

    *Incentive to declare formalities even if anonymous to other citizens

Establishing Principal

Abundance Principal

Within the fulfilling of criteria, operational vigor changes focus into assumed refinement, or enhancement phase, refocusing criteria of abundance in relevancy to premise of determination/output

- Change in fuels

- Potential alteration in storage/movability needs, such as if overall needed now met for operations of a set limit/configurations

Need of indicating status, progress

Reminder that the schedule adhered of complete itself adds towards abundance in re-initiation as having potential, for good working stature

*Observation of lifelong pursuits to manage and attempt to increase an otherwise significant/insignificant role, production, and yield: preventing deliberate corruption of a vital

*Intelligence component as contextually driven

Travel Principal

- Travel routs as visited for abundance in virtue of being short status invitation

- Sample model forms as meant for public consumption, possibly of a specialized access, entry

- Good fortune intended, advertised as still requiring the visiting guest to leave as scheduled

- Tourism areas as meaning not lived into past domestic, national deadlines

- Sex services as contracted for the performance, potential banning for any returning, or far shorter a duration of living near than reserved for touristic allocation

    *Death trap allocations enabling stalking, yet resulting in death upon, at entry

- Overall Standard of no injury, do not harm given as course load within highly touristic environments lived in, and rather near from

- Orientations and empowerment summaries for those living on set, on location, mobile performance workers

** National leadership and esteemed titles as allowed to project unlimited and incredible slogans of allowance and welcome, yet still subject to doctrines signed into as long term adherence, conditioning

Travel/Tourism Principal – Performance Feedback

Establishing satisfaction standards

- Enjoyment of occupation (ranking industry performer standards

- Endurance entry, are those visiting enabling, allowing durability of operations?

  - Emergency notice of damaging activity, rescale/largescale intrusion as mobilizing counter offensive resources

- Mass moving of highly effective areas into other areas

- Overall desires to communicate firmly, yet towards the many afflicted or mighty elite (those deemed untouchable), a firm readiness to implement death traps in face of corruption

  - Flexibility of remaining hopeful and agreeable in face of any level of hostility, knowing they are being rendered extinct

  - Enabling high dangerous lure and bait position with significant fortunes for performances

  - Reminder that the status of progress Is momentary pleasure such as from relief, yet the success is technical, and not felt (predictably) unless a solutions building conclusion is moved forward with, into

  - Requirement of death trap earning to advantage to both fortify own structure and overall disfavored reasons for their implementation

  - Safety areas to fall back or into as assigned core within design

- Reminder that conditioning is an overall feature of success, for the ease of undertaking/performance

Establishing Securities

Securities Performance Consideration (meditative insight)

Meditative reflections as a tribute to sensitivities in relation to evaluating progress/development as historical referencing, biologically driven

- The ability to performance and prove supreme (worthwhile)

- The withdrawing into, from, forming self for the performance of victory

- Recognition of self within the advancing through weakest attributes into fortified, success driven formulation/criteria-driven (including as retiring)

Securities Targeting Automated – Emergency Status

- Line of sight across groups of four for targeting

    o A measure of speed in determination of movement across the line

    o A measure of elevation or decent as gridding the line

    o A super imposed capture view, to measure movement per adjustments (multi layered)

    o A measure of thickness, assumed armor in determination of priority targeting using lines (Triangle moving, filled across line)

    o Movement of several line groups as covering various angels as highlighted priority in targeting (hexagon)

    o Note of any symbols on those targeted as high priority, to search for other lone high priority

    o Search of faces from targeting to identify spouse, children family

    o Warning on groups forming in lines to back away from grounds

    o Duration of formations covering every angles as itself a reason to highlight, such as of men, women, children, animals, object barriers

    o Death trap as fake as in associated to control over-ride to change, alter durations of monitoring

Securities Targeting Automated – Alerted status
- Anxiety monitoring as crowds shrieks, commotion in voices

- Public speaking, confirmation of permissions

    o Finding, guiding a person scheduled to perform to a given location specified

    o If applicable, status update to nearby securities notifying performance ongoing, and how to guide anyone asking where

    o Possible preparation od nourishment, such as per benefits, or privileges of access

        ▪ Performer

        ▪ Crowds

    *In relation to schedule of performance, break time allocated

Securities Consideration
- Accomplishment validates enjoyment, replenishing as eating, drinking, feasting, individually or collectively

- Instinct as to stop moving completely at sign of trouble, as having to be told to go, or please go.

- Those not afflicted, not harmed better predisposed to lend a helping hand

- Sight of blood may cause people to stop, unwilling to proceed further until further instructed

- Mismatched or misplaced food is a sign of oddity, concern

Securities Targeting Automated – Respect Status

- Adding a square on each person so that the square extends beyond the person and if the squares bounce into each other, there is a lack of personal space (indicator)

- Adding square to differing objects and note highlighted issues from their proximity

    - Waste management

        - Items falling out of containment

    - Wild Animals

        - Trajectories

    - Unsupervised children

        - Speed of play chaotic

    - Movement

        - Speed of people chaotic

            - Followed by running as alerting caution to those running into scene

Wisdom Accumulator

- Discerning between the quality of things as calculating default durability

    o Creating reference images and comparing within time span of days, weeks, months, years

        ▪ Discoloration Indicator

        ▪ Power outages/light modification

            • Circle on light sources, notification if circle area no longer providing light in contract to outside circle

        ▪ Associating rate of discoloration with product performance

        ▪ Highlighting recommendations by contrasting results per weather formula

            • Rainy

            • Freezing weather

            • Humid weather

            • Wind and particles erosion

Wisdom Accumulator – Measurements
- Measures of weight

  - Transportation usage of fuel

  - Weight vs. replacement need of materials (background measure)

  - Weighing of populations visiting

  - Weighing population in relation to food types, themes

    - Frequency and weight as anonymous readings

  - Weighing based on physical labor

  - Weighing based on physiological related events (assumes semi anonymous membership plans)

  - Supplies centered verifications (semi anonymous as alerting, checking for loss)

Tracking Trajectories – Connecting Securities Targeting automated
- Origins of paths by lines, angles of entry

- Actions relate to standard disruptions per industry, career, function-based principal

  - o Supreme structure as having image, job description references

    - Difficult tasks as highlighted, solutions building quick learn

    - Readying system references for known issues of tasks, forwarding to human resources as applicable content for learning

    - General befitting reinforcement to work, such as beautification potential

      - Civics area ready for usage potential

      - Pledge based contributions noting (faith, conditioning programs)

      - Aid to wild life from securities alert, notice to animal related incentive groups

  - Highlighting groups formed due to presence of passer by

  - Potential artistic allowance for walls, such as voted in by locality

    - o Submitting criteria, creating competitive prizes

Instruction Principal

- The reminder of long term consequence as invoking imagination of subjective trauma in realization of ignorance predictable as becoming (is disrespect) off purpose/dysfunctional

   - The elevation of ignorance as freedom from misconfigurations of a lost self/worth esteem

   - The quickness of punishment, becoming the quickness of longer termed regret, than that of resolution as typical, accumulative and becomes perspective/momentum of thought

*A calculation of purpose/result, vs. the predictable investment of time and energy

   - The amount of patience the instructor or student will-have/should-have

      - Agreements/disagreements between man and woman

Solutions Rendering

- Patience towards ignorance not imposing violations as exercise

- Avoidance of advantage per predictability of regret

- Bound by ignorance as having to wait for permissions of context to regret therein

- Separating fast movement targets found from still or slow moving crowds, especially in relation to membership, criteria zones, in relation to alterations in peaceful formations

   o Sudden movements within, adjusting crowds as indicator

   o Locking onto metal or other objects as default persons

      ▪ Assumes persons in origins, overlapping communications sources finding

Usage as security Targeting

- Supply routes

- Borders

- Reserved public spaces

- Membership areas (assumed privilege)

- Mobile setup

- Privet walkaways (voted for, membership)

- Mountains

- Streams

- Areas with injury frequency

- Areas with known weather disruptions

- Areas with wildlife population

- Areas were repeated amounts of blood sighted

- Honors privilege

- Authoritative areas

- Resistance fighting areas

- Artistic performance areas (such as singing)

- Capital regions (elite business scheduled ongoing)

- Defensive war allocation

- Advancing wisdom

Select Targeting

- Hunting specific targets

- Gates, Entrances

- Leadership figures

  - Record of all searches by ID asking, confirmed by layered security facility entry

  - Increased sensitivity to encirclement, rapid movement, abrupt movement

    - Sensitivity as reduced leeway for non-obedience

    - Sensitivity as elimination of any form approaching, breaching, intruding

    - Sensitivity as evaluation of securities as threat

    - Sensitivity as removal of special interest or elite status from programed protection

Select Targeting – Emergencies Maneuvering

- Movement towards favored locations as reinforced or near verified transportation

- Extending reference basis as cycling through public, of social media and other stated public sentiment by individuals among crowds

- Removal of weak securities persona form the area, casual sounding, quick replacement of heavy fortification if mobile timing applies

- Addition of roadblocks, filtered allies (assumes immediate mobile transition possible)

- Emergencies trained as priority guarding positions

- Momentary emergency power allocations for defensive enforcement

    o Setup of defensive grids, where people can be setup defensively against any and all approaching endangerment

    o Defensive advance as attack lines, defensive engagement parameters moving forward with target with emergency protections

    o Examination of casualties for common employers, notification of power structures such as company organizations, groups, and membership involved. Is there an inner racial, bloodline relevancy therefrom

    o Taking note of anyone arriving on scene complicating situation (including equipment issues)

Select Targeting – Theft

- Targeting property for changes in condition

- Targeting protection status individuals for movement nearby, of others hunting or war instruments

- Targeting labor demonstrations for internal or external others causing provocation

- Targeting of wild life for others imposing theft

- Targeting capital region assets for alterations as significant movement

    o Significant as out of shape used in overlay confining image/shape/target into/for purposes of static conformity (Targeting in determination of invalid approaches)

    o Hexagram with dot, circle in center as locked onto asset labeled target due to being viewed, monitored, under surveillance

Hexagram Applications

- Creating distance to leadership policies as indicating honest sympathy (deserving, demonstrated)

- Requirement of space between criminals, as spacing policy

- Indicating casualty or decapitated, as not having moved beyond boundary of hexagon from center as original position (such as measuring non movement, determining static resolve)

- Determining games or sports victory at momentary actions (too quick to see, requires confirmation), or vigor (determination for victory rising)

- Partial hexagon usage as over-layer of goal/point area, and making center circle instrument of usage crossing hexagram line

- Using hexagram to determine jumping points in relation to a maximum height threshold, maintaining image to background ratio as (measured, calibrated) approach perspective

- Determining animal enthusiasm as movement in relation to centered within hexagram

- Hexagram on those stated comments unclear, such as to examine influence of confusion, uncertainty, error

- Hexagram on reported issue to show development of issue, such as in material form, or changes in colorations as standard indicator/highlighted

Moderation Formula

- Establishing a bottom to rise from, and thereby a top (Using applicable shapes possible formed, recognized)

- Establishing weak and strong in relevancy to a criteria measurement equating such as color shade of majority vs discoloration

- Establishing peaceful as bound within acceptable routes, localized privacy accords, regulated noise allowance vs. excess such as prolonged or ongoing disruptive as out of boundary, as exceeding regulations

  o Consideration of past frequency of occurrence

  o Consideration of duration

  o Consideration of recognized noise involved

  o Movement within a fixed area, such as personal or hospital bed movement therein within frame of hexagram as measuring movement within/across lines therein

  o Use of hexagram/hexagon in relation of a marriage contract and the approach of others, such as to disengage possibilities of romance

  o Guarding guests from unwarranted, unwelcome, or unauthorized approach, touching, petting

  o Measuring of prosperity by examining amount of space filled with luxury or valued items within shaping of inventories (of images, dimensions) categorized by select rooms/themed-rooms across differing household, buildings, emplacements

  o Calculating point of travel stay with walkable/transportations in relevancy to desired locations of interest, to vitals considered imperative (assumes personal matrix attached to conform personal preferences, market valued esteems binding considered)

  o Defense policies setup in connection to hexagon/hexagram usage to determine mobility, entrance, travel, exist of sights reserved for targeting (active aiming in preparation to defend/attack)

  o Restocking based on volumes in areas monitored in relevancy to decline and therein initiating restock, refreshment

    ▪ Eating areas

    ▪ Refreshment tables

    ▪ General objects needed stocked

Powerful as Confident

Powerful as enjoying the moment (implies self and environmental control). Using monitoring to catalog spacing arrangements, inventories therein, happiness in context to similar applicable themes, and premises

Powerful as simulating in solutions building only, conclusive material formed for material in the usage of creation/expansion to:

> **Infrastructural Additions, Modifications**
>
> **Records/Archives** (reference building per categories of relevancy)
>
> **Management of Holdings** (Technologies/resource support preparation for trends as traditional)
>
> **Forms** (inventory and easy usage of forms to overlap differing selectable layers of display, including durations of in-effect
>
> o   Settings as privileges, access relevant
>
> > ▪   Emergency settings conflict warning

Communications: Data-Centers
Supreme Network Defaults

Intended relevant per supreme powers as structured in Systematic Faith:

Education Supreme

Media Supreme

Production Supreme

Faith Supreme

Justice Supreme

Political Supreme

Military Supreme capped as internal system only, network to base camp administrations only.

Communications Standard

Distinguishing formalities between public and privet, and enabling their discourse in an

Organized professional manner

- Creating subject titles, premise per entry being discussed as self-moderator

- 2 Minuit discussion intervals

    - Group options to red flag breach/derailment of premise/subject discussions

    - Intended reflecting of good outcomes

    - Easy print/forward cue card formats

- Discussion phase as segregated for ease of function

    - Formalities and Introduction phase

    - Evaluation/explanation of operations and system performance standard

    - Modification as intervention and acknowledging if prioritization in process generation

        - Case by case as benefiting from a mapped exemplary

    - After usage recap/emergency recap if permissions allocated

- Potential vote in structure as long in anywhere, vote from limited, set, already agreed upon structure of options/solutions

System Wide Communications Standard

- Travel relevant summery updates

- Alerting of politically derived policy shifts

- Curtesy communications reminding of schedules, specific rules or codes of conduct intended conformed to

- Administration keeping in mind conflicts and issues in the area arising, such as civil unrest, festive opportunity

- Transportation updates or reminder of no allowance on changing transportation

- Emergency line for severe doubt in question

Embassy as system hub
(Facilitation central) operating movements, client cases for)

- Hospital, presumed operations and performance

- National missions: Candidates confirmation & training

- Intelligence: Evaluation of refugee claims

- Freelanced consultations opportunities

- Other visas relevant, short term, mid length in term, and function based

Strategic Determination/Communications

- Formal structure to filter and prioritize incoming communications

- Basis for approval rating, what elements are meaning measured approved, and are those responsible themselves approved (approval ratings)

- Highlighting where performance is most approved, such as within public performance or it's organization such as speech writing

Credentials Evaluation

- Meeting formal criteria objectives

- Establishing challenges in which the impression can be measured, such as by would-be co-workers

- List of formal decisions possible with potential commentary validating choice

- Means to audit bribes, sexual gratuity, and gifts non-conforming to company/organizational-formalities, relevant expectations

- Record of denials

    - Regional

    - Industry specific Listed

- Clear privacy rights/freedoms listed

- Clear strategies for approaching sensitive issues/historically conflicted situations/persons

    - List of themes or content specific

- Each supreme structure as having leeway besides the ideological core (Integrity) itself required supported, centered upon

*Invalidation of any information gained from breaching locations such as based on privacy allocations, securities

- Use of specialized background music/user-specific-encoding created to identify privacy protect areas, such as protected per person, group, event

Opportunities Platform

- Adding introductory or overall lesson-plan or lecture format information establishing desired contextual approach/strategy/operational formation

- Listing members approved or required attendance

- Potential requirement out of overall pool of events, such as recapping overall all events at end per event as optional remain, stay, snacking/refreshment

National Special Representation Organization - Formal Social Platform

- Approved directly per structural power

- Contains protocols, guidelines for emergency response, international aid support objectives as options allowed per conflict/disaster

- Guidelines for networking authoritative measures such as recruiting entire segments of population using communications applications

    - Creating intelligence formations based on proven/approved stability (core-groups)

- Authoritative and intelligence input towards communications hub (central point facilitating) determining grievances, solutions building

- General criteria required stable for consideration of structural, developmental: energy, supportive health care to intended/proposed class function relevancy of development, regional ability to process intellectual rights, clear taxation to income distribution, and thereof public and private distribution allocations secured

- Self-filters, Audit in contradicting facilities or operational structuring such as food and sewage or hospital and morgue

- Uniforms image and validation section

- Establishing dialect, language (ABC's exemplified, lecture samples as industry/function based expectations) examples for recommended or quality expectation in communications

- Exemplifying implications as explaining in relevancy to strategic goals, or contractual performance criteria relevancy, as quality indicator

    - Clear highlighting of guidance vs. establishing observation, remarks, feedback

Public Relations
Action Consequence Feedback Portal

- Exemplifying (maps, presentations) demonstrating values of previous strategies through results as predicted, and results otherwise occurring

- Examining for carefully crafted contradictory rhetoric, such as given out to common people yet required specialized, professional viewpoint to interpret and correct

- Enabling media content to quickly explain complex social occurrence as relevant to a supreme category, or in relevancy to its structures such as if affecting the template awareness projected by systematic faith (Integrity formulation along/across archives, systems, supreme and stellar books: judgement core), as universally bound/alarming

- Exemplifying, explaining calendar events, scheduled undertakings made formally available for public consumption

- Promoting the sales/purchasing of this work as template/doctrine of principal, establishing roles conformity

- Maintaining a website presence

Establishing Convention

- The mindful organization of guidance as set forth in template accord/fashion, in distribution to a system embedded with potential filtrations and other assumed quality assurance component at, including identifying measurement, and results from concludes towards direction/redirection affirming premise, as mechanically prescribed/attainable (a work tool application)

- As function based, the differing avenues/segmentation of specialization are thereby strategized within outlines, establishing a commonality of guidance whose parallel to education is in the attention and intention to intellectual pursuits of development, vis a vis the status of existence as technologically bound

- Practical, as in determination of establishing short term as considered theories and long term as considered projects whose core is judgement, from a cultural, unified stance assembly

*These standards as establishing what is satisfactory, and thereby establishing what assures the self, individual in conformity to having, being part of a destiny

- Assumes destiny and the comprehension of destiny is paramount to self-conclusion, therein emotional reinforced as a constructed of mindful approach/operations, and outlook thus establishing convention, and being deprived of such attention to detail

Staff/Workers/Selected Participants
Orientation, Lessons, Lecture, seminars

Readying for duty as gaining access to active duty performance schedule

- Aid status as requiring specific information

    - Unlocking access

    - Unlocking locational and privilege details

- Trained Status

    - Weapons and defence status active (Upgrade to upgrade weapon usage)

    - Diplomatic training as drama, scenario building

- General upgrade potential as program benefit for select regional settings

    - Assumes advanced professional minds may adapt into securities from natural talents found

        - Potential need to have anonymous yet registered ID due to family/regional ties

            - Potential increase in resources embedded, purchased asset benefits

            - Potential family allowances and transferable if as gift-only

            - Potential allowance as criteria based offers

General Principals

- That abstract considerations formulate as to integrate principal, a mechanism to bypass emotional considerations itself meant to bypass, thus the biological disposition/organization of system awareness/comprehension, an acute desire itself cultivated into form/being, structures layered and complex as reinforcing

- That attention is given to merit withstanding own occupation or in aims of the trajectory of others, thus are lesson plans relatable to function based conclusion, yet being layered require both an ease and a structured adherence generally conforming to principals of compatibility, innovation, and conclusive oversight

- Lower faculties, as led, tends to be associated to that which is rendered automated, which is already cared for or supplied, of that which seems to involve pre-existing fulfillment and completeness, and thereby is relative to the overall structure and system, and one's place of prestige/access or power/resourcing therein

- Higher faculties, as leading, tend to involve the creative, adaptive development of fulfilling, completed systems whose very form thus adds itself onto the lower faculties as an esteem towards elevation, symbolic of betterment, an ascension of purpose through cognitive design/safekeeping/performance

- Lower and higher faculties being themed in comprehension of social culture's ability to embrace individual will towards the determination of guidance

- Thereby the examples one gives must generally include themselves, as realistic accord to patriotic loyalties of a realistic status of insight

- Thereby involvement in the system as for mutual gain involves a series of long term and short term expectations, conclusion, and refinements

- Thereby self-refinement and collective or social refinement manifest in a culture of manifest will per destiny in direction to self-conclusion (proposed ideally as in God's Direction)

- Thereby, the reinforcing of conclusions is itself protected and or defended in virtue of the system's awareness, understanding, and as influenced/validated, causing ideal stance to clash with corruption invading through false social strife where the empowerment of the individual becomes manipulated into the tyrannical application disregarding general principals by falsifying accords, observations, conclusion, and thus corruption as any measure and its consequence

Symbolic Convention

Festive mentions as meaning:

- Virtuous acts of celebration as holding with integrity feature compatible to regional, custom faith, systems, civics, supreme such as this text as doctrine assumed included, and staller

- Faith symbols as defended, approved by reserves of image, such as in relation to premise and formality of membership or invitations compatible

- Dogma expectations as involving practical features/virtues: concentrated self-control acclaimed, durable ceremonial performance, and the demonstration of bonds that promote interaction yet secure distinction including adding or not adding special interest members into ceremonies and instead adhering to formations/formal configurations tending to be vital, scheduling and a safeguard against corrupting groups coordinating their own agenda

- As meaning, those performing are intended well known, rehearsed, pulled out for not conforming, not allowed to their mourn, over-excited or be dazed into changing ceremonial appearance

Science as Symbolic Convention

- Proposing projects and developments for scientific pursuits as medicine, simplified means of noting acceptability

- Assigning leeway of vagueness if formally an artistic enhancement as experimental attachment (assumed co-dependant)

- Displaying the development of scientific pursuits, branches, with potential recollection of the abstract nature connecting faith, abstract speculation, and sketched of observed yet barely understood to euphoric visions/glimpses of innovation/inventions (displaying onto an order of operations resembling scientific pursuit, further refined as in limitations of systematic awareness: bound within integrity deemed essential)

- Education having to specify and adapt per audience whose position within development is a projected timeline of insight, as meaning the era and time of mention and of content mentioned are contextual and can be varied as optional.

- A scientific vital consider universally important, can have differing contextual explanations and examples, such as across the supreme structure of power

* Education Supreme, Media Supreme, Production Supreme, Faith Supreme, Justice Supreme Political (Capped as Panel) Supreme, Military Supreme (capped as internal system)

- The science of military (biological engineering) should enable gymnastics-able as considered a dynamic achievement of material fibre

- Ability of movability, flexibility as defining feature of compatible to our intelligent form/image

- Complex system of voluntary and involuntary systems for movement in connectivity to cognitive foresight

- Establishes where strength is limited for breeding, and may need to change breeding program to facilitate

- Development of prosthetics thereby not complete until dexterity possible, relocation into more mobile, technological placement recommended as

Resource Sanctuaries

(Invite only, presumed to train, create, or display to members exclusive content)

- Research asset

- Laboratory

- Model

- Gymnastic

- Auditorium for vocal arts

- Specialty lockers/storage

- Specialty shops (such as automated pay and pick-up, pay and open, retrieve)

- Booking/forwarding-quest for display rooms, gallery space benefits (access-privilege)

- Booking lecture rooms

- Booking Meeting rooms

- Housekeeping arrangements attached (subject to fees, level of privileged access assumed

- Booking for classes of luxury: kitchen, serving areas, service

- Auto arrangement for secured transportation, such as from workshop or lab to display and or storage

    - Self packing supplies

Institutional Network Platform
Members Resource

Intended for councils

- Academic Papers

- Contributions

- Discussions

*Highlighting portions of text of media and signalling what is non-conforming as to require authors or related members to explain, further detail, or remove contents

    - Subjected to votes such as to validate or invalidate criticisms and responses

*Integrity allocation as meaning if the subject matter does not conform to integrity formulation veto potential from Acari Systems as host

    - Exceptions possible using system works as reference material supportive of adding biological framework as source for determination of God's image, as required nevertheless in compatibility to network status/adherence

Culture as Cultivation

- Appropriate function as required fees for unproductive, game-like playing on site

(If you don't belong there, you pay for the inclusion as without penalty of playing)

*Members should have inventories that show own merit at any moment of any work complete

    - Based on results or otherwise criteria based

- A requirement of a logical predisposition to character

    - Mourning not except from being trouble maker

    - Mental inability from fatigue or unprepared may be grounds for exclusion

    - Proof of performance may be required if no inventory relates to field of expertise

- Play leeway potential relating to gaming and cannabis as religious right and technological oversight accorded

    - Grounds, being irritated by others/seeking atonement

- Children not necessarily admissible to location (registered care packages/benefits)

- Potential language or accents requirement

- Potential privileged leeway for furnishing, funding, being asked to service (accomplished workers/performers/specialists) relevant to the location, as lifetime benefit potential

> - Assumes by invitation only remains of limited scheduled event as procedure driven

> - Operational norms complying

> *Donations must request, be granted specific access privileges signed into, otherwise site intended secured from so called pay backs

> - Potential grants in form of access-privilege, and use of resources on location

> *Grants excluded from being transferred

> *Grants as requiring criteria, requirements, obligations attached/accessible

Nationalist Accords Platform
(Work Relevancy)

- Organized acceptability as united by principal adhering a vision towards/of positive achievement

- Embedding filters to project a stable traditions premise for alignment of members

> - Updating directives to members yet reaffirming the premise as standard of compliance, compute

- Labor organized to promote performance of duty as specified by determination to stabilize, adapt as efficient

> - Assumes contributions are made by completed systems such as from completed succession of performance accumulated/experienced, and or trained

- Able to bypass political conformities if mentioned counters established premise signed in by totality of formal political agency

> - Assumes national front worthwhile, organized, excels

> - Potential indicator to reorganize, move to better locations nationally

> - Requires platform where criteria and logged training/experience is thus accessible/attainable

- Troubleshooting requires an open mind, understanding of the problem
- Endurance to situations as trained status, training criteria

- Potential sanctuary status on workshop, as do not disturb to members

- Potential bypass list, enabling family/secretarial status

- Benefits signed into vs. wages assigned

- Archives Section - Historic mentions in purpose of cleanse and glorify

- Transferring inventories equipment workloads into museum/exposition status

- Rendering inventories storage/archives complete, access as do not tamper

- Potential workshop inventory manifest as if taken apart log new projects

- Potential pay to access, status required to access as custom capitalist adjustments

- Assumes a return towards administrative category, division to foresee expansion requirements/ability

- Potential assignment towards youth training/ band from youth/non-specialist status involvement

- Potential reservations, as paid for secured

- Direct notification (to registered owner) at time of request to enter/breach

- Potential negotiations automated as, wait and pay/do/achieve less to attain benefit

- Potential ban on access until proven ability to construct, design, fabricate as nevertheless (delicate, fragile)

- Call to study unknown forces, phenomenon at a given location, operations

- Development/advancing of methodology

- Potential racially based as in relevancy on the acceptability to conforming to faith programs as conditioning agency molding physical properties of people in the long term, in conformities to formal doctrine/guidelines thereby establishing template/direction

- Assumed same civics, supreme, and staller as establishing seeming class divisions of expected behaviours, cultivation of taste, and public appearance

Apprentice Programs
National Accords Platform (Work Relevancy)

- Expectation of duties

- Logging in exact status, personal obligations such as to family members

- Creating exact timeframes of participant expectations based on initial entry of personal data

- Potential ban of recruiters or converters from bothering the visiting participant

> - Potential need to list all so called impure tendencies in relation to potential culture clashes foreign

> - Arranging for compatible locations of practice play, devotions

- Potential easement, securement of localized custom training sub-program as expansion to

Training/Operational/Occupational Programs

Training/Operational/Occupational Criterial - National Accords Platform (Work Relevancy)
- Is the contract for intellectual, social, physical ability?

> - With consideration each have peer groups adjusted/participating in specific lifestyle and habits conforming to industrious ability/knowledge

> - Protection from corrupt foreign locals trying to immediate non relevant or non-related industry/workers

- Potential easement, securement of localized custom training sub-program as expansion to apprenticeship programs

> - To promote integrity as default as embedded values expected universal

> - To enable esteem for the occupation being developed, expanded into the region as having nevertheless sound judgement in broadcasting in relation to regional culture, and historical implications thereof

- Establishing role model per level of qualified training, or focusing on developmental phases coherent to the training process being instructed/cultivated into physical familiarity, intellectual recollection, and profession embedding of personal efficiencies configurations (tools/equipment/supplies & organization, lifestyle arrangements, support structure as applicable)

Invitations Platform
Operatlonal Options Standard

Per Supreme Structural Power

- Hearings

- Negotiations

- Witness Public state as assumed reasonable, optional (Survey)

- Events Participation

    - Attendance for/by function as/of attending required to service specific assigned/chosen tasks

- General feedback, assumed privileged access as relevant criteria reached as specialist, authority, function

- Membership orientated conference/workshop event

- Usage of specialized office resource, assumed self-contained

- Potential leeway for submitting to a testimony/confession

- Returning to clarify discussion highlights

    - Potential expiration of entry/access-privilege if no reply addition given

- Status reports on overcoming challenges, meeting criteria, fulfilling requests

- Potential Mobile/Transit Allocations

- Highlighting special allowances as green as active

- Highlighting boring, pointless story-like as meaningless comparing, tired metaphors, (as orange)

- Highlighting sever contradictions, such as to overall convention or strategic formation, (as red)

- Availability indicator for live or scheduled appearance/performance

- Filters within options to forward as requiring both to have access-privilege verified

    - Automatic print out of limitations and responsibilities attached to documents

    - Quick formatting solutions, options for different modes of application, if applicable

    - Potential viewing logs, stated as logged/access-monitored content

- Listing points of access, relevant broadcasting links

- Formal representations invitations summery and invite options

- Assumed qualifying to be emplaced in the civics structure

- Charities opportunities/proposed criteria based objectives

- Predicative health and recovery directions/feedback

- Checking for updates across all linked databases

- Safety, transitional locations, such as sanctioned as function based relocation programs

- Heritage programs

- Permissions granting area, what, who, can send invitations of nevertheless filtered through membership status databases

Opportunities Survey of Regional Populations

- Supreme structure of power's frameworks and their general range of coverage

(Faith, Political panel, Military, Justice, Media, Production, Education)

- General parameter based on registered industry, and trades professionals

- General Parameter of all eased transportation serviced, especially if offered in connection to a network of service

- Associated investment in advertising, including associated domestic groups in connectivity

- Accessing different levels as per authoritative privilege of participation/membership

- General salary expectations/requirements per cost of living

- Assumed secured facilities required

- Alert on overcrowding

- Alert on incoming mass crowding

    - Potential stop on all incoming transportation

    - Potential mass mobilization to exit area

        - Alert on all mobilized transportation being blocked/purchased/otherwise no longer active collectively

- Accessible manuals of interpretation

- Not meant to be transferable, nor rentable nor for mass relocation

- Intended to secure ongoing vital areas required for overall stabilization of domestic progress

- Free facilities and general purpose allocations should by area and must by overall area, be blocked by walls, barriers and filtering means of mobility prevention from secured site

- Area not to receive state awards or allowances for feel good, or politically correct yet paid for by state funding beyond thereby what is formal, on premise and allocated

    - Meaning augmented salaries and secured areas themselves assumed state funded

        - Promotes or requires community support and membership purchasing into select detailed plans of activity

    - Assumes secured status means everything has to be planned in advance

    - Assumes overcoming fairness issues, requires paying

Information: Vital Infrastructure & Special Developmental Interest

Room/Floor/Building access to (panel/information-terminal)

- Supportive literature

- Research on the development as a process

- Relevant traditions and ancient contributions

- Proposals as projections and predictions display

- Respecting boundaries of privet, vs. official functions

- Projects platform

- Institutional platform

- Cross-referencing

- Public awareness information-pool

  - Assumed educational as per structure of power

- Core methods, staff evaluation, orientation design - control

- Premise mapping

- Locations mapping

- Status monitoring, age, expected deprivation,

- Admissions, testing, program choice

- Resource mapping

- Departments/content structuring, mapping

- Areas and territories under control/covered by, per structures of power

  - Color coded

  - Display of multi accessed personnel

  - Level of education/training predictably required at location (color coded easement)

  - Level of function based status, or trained at locations (color coded easement)

  - Level and premise of clearance (color coded easement

Formula/Formulation

In reflection to ideal as judgement core, the attachment of a traditions as main attaching segment, is the proposed enhancement as such:

Quality as Durability: Ideal

Quality as per functionality in centralized: Ideal, and component support: Traditions

As Ideal: Functional Tradition – As Support: Traditions Functional

(Inner complimentary inversion)

Such as: Doing/Being

               Practice/Guidance   *As intelligence administration/formation: Guidance as doing

                                       *Therefore as complete/core: Guidance as being

Doing	Being	Being/Doing
Social Clubs	Inclusion and civics detachment	
Conceptual configurations	Traditions building and overall configurations selection	
Universality	Doing and Being	and being/doing
Conformity and scale	Compatibility mechanized and scale relevancy	
Hierarchy and glorification	Function based class and admiration/cultivation	
Individuality and destiny	Practice and guidance	and guidance/practice
Destiny and Divinity	Direction and status	
Updating, merger	Popular and adaptive	
Abstraction and reason	Formulation and purpose	
Duality and mutual-reinforcement	Considerate and expanding interested	
Gender	Masculine, Feminine, Objective	

Core of function / Function as Core:

- Survival
- Specialist
- Operational
  - Maintenance/Repair
  - Upgrade/Self-determination: Objective summery

Core of Principal

(Refinement, filters quality self-assessment)

- Archives of doubts
- Original elaborations in relation to traditions as function based reference building
- Proving, building/operating custom template
    - Determination/limitations
        - Resource anticipation, exploration, analysis
            - Expansion per overall consideration of objective/determination network

Prime as central, whose supportive tradition is set as default to ideal as control

Thereof, detachment and self-reliance of traditions as by default, securing prime/control.

Does traditions divide prime, or rather that prime as functioning is in relevance to system status, reaffirming system integrity as paramount/national-bypass configurations: Core 0.

Traditions as Group Forming

- Display lab/work-station per group function
- Display lab/work-station per individual
    - Groups Assigned
    - Groups developing as challenging
    - Groups working live
    - Groups working per industry

Healthy (based on functionality) equates into

Health...............................Ecology/Environment

Beautiful (Safeguarding the deciphering of sensual stimuli)

Beautiful............................Figure/Form

Loving (Aligning emotion reaction with idealistic instigation)

Loving..............................Sensibility

Dignified (Safeguarding relationships, interaction)

Dignified............................Standards

Productive (Safeguarding ideals promotion of: procreation, individual proficiency, profession)

Productive----------------------------Career

Civilized (Providing a supportive infrastructural means aligned to ideology)

Civilized..............................Facilitation

Truthful (Accuracy of depiction, accumulation of knowledge)

Truthful...............................Archives

(Regional)----------------------------(Connected)

Faithful (Affirmation of understanding / enhancement of sensual- emotional self-actualization)

Faithful..............................Pledges

(Custom)----------------------------(Complete)

Wholesome Systematic values promoting integrated functionality

Wholesome..........................Secured

(System)...(Securities)

Ideal---Destiny

Faith……………………………………….Natural Intelligence

Civics…………………………………….Steller

Political------------------------------------ Wilderness Adaptive

Integrity--Judgement-Core

Such as: Doing/Being

                 Practice/Guidance   *As intelligence administration/formation: Guidance as doing

                                        *Therefor as complete/core: Guidance as being

Practical – Communal (Day to Day)	Guiding - Eternal (Forever, Always)	
Doing	**Being**	
Social Clubs	Inclusion and civics assignment/operations	
Conceptual configurations	Traditions building and overall configurations selection	
Universality	Doing and Being	and doing
Conformity and scale	Compatibility mechanized and scale relevancy	
Hierarchy and glorification	Function based class and admiration/cultivation	
Individuality and destiny	Practice and guidance	and practice
Destiny and Divinity	Direction and status	
Updating, merger	Popular and adaptive	
Abstraction and reason	Formulation and purpose	
Duality and mutual-reinforcement	Considerate and expanding interested	
Gender	Masculine, Feminine, Objective	

Being Judaic, as technological application of faith, as having judgement-core

Doing Judaic, as involving self into technological continuity, remaining within the image of intelligence able to preserve network status/reasoning/appreciation

Being Systematic Faith, as universal to all faith bound, pledged into the All Mighty
Doing systematic Faith, as complete systems of inner compatibility, of formal specialization and function-based access and privilege abridging ideals of integrity

Being healthy/conservative: As guiding reasonable in terms of inner intellectual design onto outwards will as per referenced and resource (access, privilege relevant)

Doing health/conservative lifestyles: Facilitating as adaptive/steadfast individuals, adaptive/function-premise family, governance adaptive/stable policies, faith as long term/networked cultivation

Being/Doing systematic Order: Establishing ideals in projection of a uniting destiny whose measure is an example/model as integrity. The civics, political adaptive towards the universally stabilizing integrity as ideal. Thereby, integrity is set as primary in being, and in doing the political/civics is short term adaptive as enhancing modifier.

Metaphors as mirrored, inversion, rotating, revolving: **Dynamic with a Core.**

Being/Doing Functional:

As enhancing, the modifications are **artistic**, layered to enable insights yet in relation to a premise being proposed.

As enhancing, the **developments** (modification) are examples of worship, words as instigating the actions in accordance to a pre-existing judgement foundation/core.

As enhancing, the **conditioning** (modifications) to social interaction safeguard the formalities binding relationships whose quality is measurable by the durability of those (binding) agreements

As enhancing, **procreation** (modification) expands and secures resources for access and privilege, such as from biological advancement of predispositions, cultivation of talent, and/or overall reward from professionalism

As enhancing, **support** (modification) enables **artistry, development, conditioning**, and **procreation**, to be livable in terms of ideals of integrity as instated knowledge, known and accepted.

As enhancing, **censorship** removes corrosive elements, invasive personas against the collective importance of knowledge, removing those against an integrity basis for the determination of judgement, refinement, or as consequence to actions to instill an enhancing feature to modifications.

As enhancing, **culturing** modification is an equation of understanding/refinement, **in relevancy to support and censorship**, enabling the dexterity of using both contents towards media for understanding and categorizing depictions into controllable, emotionally driven production

Wholesome as conclusions from enhancing and modifying, updated as establishing within a continuity of/as affirmation

Being: Citizen

Doing: Patriotic

Functional   **Individual** as Freedom to Specialize

Social as Liberty to acquire capitalist gain

                   Individual & Social as facilitated by system

The measure of (civic/civil) goodness (functional/functioning) to bad (dysfunctional/malfunctioning)

As in relation to context: **formulated in determination of individual in relation to society**

As mandate (written accord signed into guidance over/as the representatives of people within the nation(s). These measures (definitions being detailed) are set as default, are taught as fundamentals, fundamental knowledge on how individuals specialize/operate and societies interpret/operate.

Fundamental: Gaining is safeguarded, durable as secured. Liberty is securement of freedom.

Thereby, freedom endures as liberty, enabling status, interconnecting perspectives, promoting culture as enhancing and naturally enables/promotes durable, beyond the baseline that is survival. Meaning brute strength is compartmentalized, as is intellectual pursuits as both are specialized, and together as collective attributes to conditioning: as per custom regional.

Civics Ideal
Functional Cultivation: Through Doing and Being

Doing (Accumulative to the status of being)

System Defaults...Experimental

Focus...Conclusive

Structured...Adaptive

*Variance within doing as using precedence, or formulating new combinations

Being (Relevant within functional determinations of doing

Wholesome as Upgrading

Clarity in relation to remaining precise

*Layered consideration within being as mindful in relation to bodily retention

Doing	Being
Promoting	Exemplifying

Can you do and be? Thereby inspiration/Inspirational

Civics Ideal in Participation to Technology

As ideal, within mechanical form, doing and being must compute/complete as functional.

The embedded configuration of an individual can be called a lifestyle, yet the specialized ability is in determination as willed, and in relevancy to resources and references.

Thereby, individuals institute mechanical form, as civilization, to enable, stabilize, and overall enhance resources and referenced, reinforcing the value, merit, obligations of determination/will.

As default, ideal, within mechanical form, doing and being must compute/complete as functional, meanwhile once stable the adaptive nature of expansion, experimentation requires formulated delicate safeguards towards innovations and self-interest.

*First the overall form is explained, and then by adding the feature that grows, the guidance matches the audience which are alive, as individuals as collectively.

Judgement-core Exemplified:

1 References considerations for Long-term as establishing securements

2 Resource considerations for Short term as adaptive, enhancing

3 System defaults long-term include leeway within being quality values establishes durability easement

4 Experimental short term segments emerge due to the adaptive living reactions therein

5 Intelligence Long-term safeguard categorization, responses securing vitals knowledge

6 Civics Short-Term enables collective choice, fortifies determination

7 Overall - The inner compatibility maintains in relation to an agreed upon structure of power, determination, adaptive as categorized into structured, diverse support

Determination-Core Exemplified

8 Inner to Overall as civics, this text, as converted for mechanical application to solidify the social diversity aspects in connectivity and compatibility to civics/civil structuring. 1-7 representing a brief of judgement-core contents, 8 representing a compliant civics determination core.

Objective Prioritization

Judgement-Core: Reference Permissions/Will

- **Premise to overall system (References)**
  - ○ Default mention of vital resources
- **Absolute Reference commands thus long term**

Premise Exemplified as/from Book 1-6 of Judgement Core

Determination-Core: Resource Data

- **Premise to market driven system (Resources)**
  - ○ Default mention of vital references
- **Absolute Resource commands thus short term (approved long term)**

Premise Exemplified as/from Book 1-7 of Judgement Core

Divinities-Core: Command/Mobilization Tactics

- **Premise to resource securement of references**
  - ○ Absolute Commands (thus securities and core culture)
- **Premise to reference securement of resources**
  - ○ Absolute Knowledge (thus core culture securities)

Premise Exemplified as/from Book 7 of Judgement Core

Objective Liberty

In terms of liberty, thereby judgement, determination and divinities are securements as functional status of an overall template securing a structure of power. The divinities is quoted as highest, yet bound to the principals of the judgement-core. Thereby, regardless how conflicting the communications, the default to is conform to integrity, which tends towards a peaceful, mindful interpretation of content/knowledge.

Liberty

Individual/Social: Harmony as conclusive, as fulfillment

Civics: Order as Performance of Duty

Divinities: Doing and Being: Amen: Completion

Doing: Individual: Refreshed to engage

Doing: Social: Solutions Building/Engaging against oppression

Doing: Civics: Duty: Constrictive/Corrective

Doing: Divinities: Projecting Destiny

Being: Individual: Liberation refreshed

Being: Civics: Performance

Being: Social: Liberation to refresh

Being Divinities: Manifest Destiny

*Integrity Refreshing (Universal)

*Measurement: Resources/References: Judgement/Determination/Fulfilment of Will

*Custom regional as meaning arranging symbolic usage in adherence to liberty

Civic Arts

Refinement of Intellectualism

- Detailing of experimental, categorized as safeguarding

Refinement of Formal Knowledge

- Science as requiring instrumentation

Refinement as Hierarchies

- Industrial as mechanical application of formulated

Refinement as Creation

- Establishing Core
- Expansion

Civic Artistic Themes

- Deliberation
- Construction
- Organization

Civic Artistic Flavor

- Influence
- Encouragement
- Captivating/Focus/Convincing

Civic Artistic Compassion

- Achievement
- Discovery
- Meaning

Artistic Continuation

- Conforming to Integrity within Ranging subjects, themes
- Relevant to a localized region
- Destination Tourism

Artistic Accreditation/Privilege/Markets-Valued (Delicate)

- Stimulation (Sense of Appeal)
- Interpretation
- Condition
- Sensual
- Nationalism (Authoritative)
- Recognized, Structural Power
- Models

Artistic Control of Access

- Age
- Licensed Restrictions
- Maturity
- Authoritative Restrictions
- Education (Comprehension)

Artistic Censor/Edification into Satire or Rendered Exemplified

Unimportance…………………………Importance
Unwarranted Opinions……………Qualified Stance
Before Freedom………………………After Freedom
Before Liberty…………………………After Liberty
Criminal Intent………………………..Civil Liberty

Criminal Abuse…………………………Civil Discussion

*Experience or Sensibility: media category and maturity rating

Artistic Safeguards

If you want controversial media approved, revise satirical consideration, maintain integrity guidance

*Guidance set in differing eras, or otherwise tested within the extreme, may require fiction status/genre

Intellectual ability of audiences has been safeguarded or tested, or technically downgraded

* Media category and maturity rating

Careful authoritative designs, blatant misuse of concept, imitation of authoritative dystopia
* Media category and maturity rating

Social programs to enable content formation

* Media category and maturity rating

Civics Academia

As pro civics, advanced intellectual arts as liberal, and science with clear funding sources, both with premise:

Categorizes relevant to funding as

Cultural Relevancy (Liberal Arts as guidance, explanations)

- Archives proving civilization
- Political proving short term
- System displaying active model and normalcy (custom regional)
- Experimental exemplifying pivotal (propose pivotal as performance)
- Empirical intelligence such as automated intelligence, designing
- Civics configurations as organized social functions
- Steller

Scientific Relevancy

Structural Powers

- 1 Media
- 2 Education (Regulating Knowledge)

...

- 1 Justice
- 2 Military

...

- 1 Production
- 2 Government

...

- 1 Civics
- 2 Faith

It could be reasoned, that from refining observation, that we may observe the structural powers as having two levels of existence, in which they relate more directly, yet as vitals are integrated require each other as a thereby structure of power.

Notice 1 is the experimental and in that manner originator of 2

Notice 2 is the source as having priorities over 1, such as within developing from freedom to securements of liberty

Notice 2 are each long term, in relation to 1

Notice 2 are more difficult to alter altogether, require more paperwork, policy, adherences, than 1

*stable/experimental of 1 is from public feedback, causing 2 to be a naturally safeguarding organization, order of operations. (Relative to the scheduling, timed nature of content)

With feedback pivotal to all levels/layers of the proposed structure of powers, safeguarding the sensibility of public conformity, conditioning of sensitivity, reinforces each area of the structural powers is essential to the overall social validity constructed, and thereby abridging judgement, determination, onto stellar in cultural relevance/affirmation of destiny.

As ideal, civics is configured to enable experience, enable measure into determination which as emotionally driven, is enabled by priorities culturing/conditioning, such as in relation to **cultural relevance** and **scientific relevancy**. Thereof, faith is included, such as faith derived the formulation enabling civics as a judgement binding to validate determination, and determination requiring judgement as foundation, intellectual support structured.

Faith was used to originate formulation found in this text as civics considerations, as industry relevant conceptual, and thereby required bound within the formulation as both conclusion to judgement and determination, and in relation to validations of own foundation/founding-purpose.

Civics Determination of Faith

- Comprehension, objective as in determination of fundamental judgement values
  - As custom regional, adhering formal doctrines of established cultural and scientific relevancy (realistic, affirming leeway of connectivity)
- Adaptive as within framework meant across vast amounts of time
- Worship as means for citizenry to explore, intentions as safe kept in consideration of integrity as judgement formula
- Conservative as civics reinforcement of faith, such as within recycling,
- Commutability of faith, as in complex, layered and similarity towards biology and technology

Civics Determination of Conservative
(Default Civics as Pro Faith Defence)

Civics Determination of Conservative, ideally, as a demonstration that governance cares about resources. Default Civics as Pro Faith Defence as an abridgement between government and production is that of an abridgement of faith and civics, and further as promoted through media and education, defended by justice and militants, as an overall systemic, layered approach of self-determination, held/strengthened by a conceptual core as indoctrinated.

With Acari as a civics means to securement, thereby data storage as sacred, keeps backups and operational knowledge concerning vitals used for, across structural powers:

- Citizen ID
- Licensing Information/Registration
- Formalities of facilities
- Securements relating to physical materials, processing, storage standards
- Service descriptions and operational detail relating/promoting to increasing durability
- Arts, science and/as luxury details, such as in models developed/stored, custom regional arrangements relating to satisfying positions of authority

The technological pursuit of Acari systems, as the civics physical embodiment to this text, is that of enabling freedoms for operation in standard, relevant to technologies domestic in anticipation/direction to mobilization stellar: Yawaeh Systems.

Safeguarding of resource extraction itself, as well as methods and operational details, varies across many industries, such as onto tourism where the focus is directly upon experiences of an emotional arrangement, and either way, esteemed fashionable (assumed).

The predictably technological application, is to fabricate, maintain the environmental conditions in a manner where resources earned and resources used are calculated, yet the operational methodology are possibly highly valuable, such as for stellar performance. As (relatively) easy means to measure complex, and layered formations of operational undertaking.

*The default judgement-core reasoning, is that the projects remain within standards of health, with consideration as a system, that differing levels of potency render thus relative, the guidance thereof/therein provided.

Determination as civics focus on specialized pursuits/Interests

- Specialist industrial development as civics secured activities encouraging physical, intellectual labors
- Family cultivation of individual formations as encouraging physical, intellectual labors
- Tourism, service industries as providing/specialized in retrieve
- Custom reginal sensuality dedication as stability through organization, experimental
  - Contracting intellectual, physical secured judgment, as well as securing in terms of registration of facilitation of intellectual, physical secured determination

Determination as Civics Professions

- Resources reminder from civics that citizens do more than preform functions, they are cultivated and conditioning into layers of awareness, fulfillment, and encouraged into satisfaction
- Securing layers of industrial knowledge, livelihood across transformative upgrades to the infrastructure, especially within upgrading vitals
  - Upgrading the baseline defaults by providing options to work into, towards legacy (founding personas) figures
  - Being mindful other regions of the world require transitions of progress that require large scale development layers of reinforcing, supportive construction such as adapted to their regional resources as custom-rendering

Determination as State Configurations

- Creating short term political activation sequences where collective development plans attached to political motto being elected, enable democratic determination
- Reinforcement that survival of the technologically proficient requires a default amount of resources that as set within defaults of configuration, are elevated within the satisfactions of liberty, in which the political promise to prioritize emerging developmental cycles in conformity to an organized, coherent, compatible as reasonable.
- Voicing affirmations (requirements) in relation to reason and integrity (judgment) as to demand, vote into action determination towards extreme
- Status of leading within a multinational arrangement, reinforces technological vitals as at emergency level in relation to non-leading nations, whom may by contrast have lax views, considerations, and thereby can, should be approached with long term power-resource plans for the ameliorations enabling stellar conformities of a nevertheless centralized within civics arrangements.
  - Meaning trying to develop other regions into the leading nation's current conformity, is not possible (predictably), by the time the projects are built, the lead is already onto new generations of versions of adaptability, such as from diversified operations enhancing.
    - If the outwards development is not an enhancing feature, then such as through political, yet secured by state configuration, expansion is slowed or blacked until compatibility is restored/established

-

-

Civics Determination as State Configurations

Integration vs. Edification

- General requirements to older doctrines be adhered to, with integrity doctrines as lead filtering potential, such as by introducing ne layers of structural power to finally organized, process and operate all kinds of task and performance requirements their old paperwork cannot comply with
- Civics censorship defaults as art over graffiti, pro nationalism as structural powers allocated default gaming, media,
- Inner structural powers reserved usage, such as bound by formalities therein, exemplifying operational standards, offering collective insights, favoring appeals to civics determination
- Determination of civics as attempted beyond judgement, meaning judgement is adhered to, and projected destinations, destiny as long term and short term evaluated through enhanced performance

Civics Determination as Culture

- Technological pursuit as the esteem to what liberty is, as defining cultural perspective
    - Integrity bound as ecologically bound/sound
- Forging trade policy, as well as corporate and business incentives along projected and fulfilled traditions building to enhance domestic as capital technical lead interest
- Media driven as promoting essential to life, liberty resolutions
- Securities as positive affirmation of technological pursuit, a structural powers overall esteem towards a balance between/among encoding/encryption, and formalities, premise
- Securing context for the enabling of contractual formalities, such as enabling capital areas, exposition sites, networking displays as heritage areas, including centralizing areas into touristic and educational sites (or otherwise themed by structural powers and cultural relevancy) to a designated area, while working with, such as modify (as to adapt) existing surface areas to maintain or transfer commerce across/along considerations of capped market values
    - Change of fabrics and redevelopment into much larger areas, as meaning relative size and importance equates substantial move (potential state moving benefit for mass development as well as buy in features for local cultural assets/productions)
- Fixing celebrations to specific building locations, projects, including scale(occupancy size) of overall area (declaring movable festivities)

Civics Determination as Upgrading

- Upgrading as feedback relevant to wellbeing, as indicator of domestic peace
    - Equities leeway as developing what persona exemplifying trends
    - Requesting contextual information in reports, or noteworthy forwarded

Capital/Social	Civics
Domestic	
Value/Demand	Establishes Reserves
Ownership Priced/Size	Survival Price Established
Luxury Price/Function	Industrial Priority Established
International-Empiric	
Commodity/Demand	Exchange Reserves
Production/Capability	Development Potential
Luxury/Trade Leeway	Reserves Potential
Steller	
Steller/Mobilization	Civics Ready

Fundamental Determination as Integrity Formulation

Conceptual Core (Premise Foundation)

Long-term Stability – Civics- Faith Reserves

Being Healthy determined as Integrity Ideals, a Systematic Approach, as meaning a framework of ideas centralized as functional in termination of overall fulfillment of categories, as it's conclusive upgrading, upkeep as the wholesome feature: The ideal framework of health as systematic awareness, as conceptual, systems basis to judgement-core.

Doing Health as (Contextually Driven)

Short Term Adaptive – Politically Driven/Applicable

Doing Healthy Determination as

- Promoting Individual and social boundaries

- Enhancing field beauty, actively within state configuration

- Esteems on fulfillment of relationship standards

- Cultivating through infrastructure as civics matter

- Faithful as samples, example, and models used within securement of healthy determination

- Safekeeping production vitals in functioning of enhancement features cultured

- Maintaining wholesome as upgrading as arising, mindful of stellar as destiny in design, conformity compute, conclude/abridge

*Individuals as in formation to lifestyles, and their relevance and in conforming to each other (civics usage, the admiration of examples as confirming to layered supports approach

* Segmented as options, elections relevant

Civics Integrity

Conclusive, Collective-Configuration/Embodiment

As universally applied/applicable, Integrity has several formation/formula. As universal, its (Integrity) ability to exist and be relevant across all judgement subject matter as a stable reference guiding measure/operations-design, then an overall configuration of, for being and doing necessitates this doctrine as covering the resources section, indicating a fortification of will version called divinities core..

Examining Integrity Formula as applicable in layers (social: judgement core, Civics: determination core, Divinity: Command, mobilization).

Healthy

Socially: That Health as fundamental extends into the significant of all ideals

Civics-Civil: That health as a leading component of judgement, applies onto all civics matters as measurable

Divine: That health has been identified as of core important to the meaning of all things/life

Beautiful

Socially: Centered on terms of health, the individuality of health reflects variance projected

Civics-Civil: That beauty relates to judgement, and is nevertheless function based literal

Divine: That the importance of beauty endures, onto, as everlasting

Loving

Socially: Interweaves judgement aspects of resource, references and determination of will core to expansion

Civics-Civil: In determination of long term self and collective cultivation plans

Divine: Enhancing depictions promoting the mobilization of virtue

Dignified

Socially: In determination of long term self and collective cultivation plans

Civics-Civil: Functions orientated as in relation to larger production formations

Divine: Enabling of automated intelligence within the formation of civics and infrastructure itself

Productive

Socially: The enabler of overall civilization as grouping of completed systems united/uniting

Civics-Civil: The facilitation of both stability and enhancing experiential

Divine: The emergence of core towards the restoration, establishing of God's direction

Faithful

Social: Long term bounds, in edification of transitional

Civics-Civil: Long term bound, displayed as short term abridgement to custom regional

Divine: An overall model, sample establishing direction

Truthful

Socially: Point of intellectual, policy maturation, status of references

Civics-Civil: Point of physical in addition to default intellectual, policy maturation, status of references

Divine: Command and mobilization as cultural, mechanically applied (universal defaults)

Wholesome

Socially: Wellbeing and in respects to upgrading

Civics-Civil: Wellbeing embedded into the default of structuring and its intelligence/perspective

Divine: A collectors of completed fulfillments, of compartmentalized adaptive

Socially: That Health as fundamental extends into the significant of all ideals

Civics-Civil: That health as a leading component of judgement, applies onto all civics matters as measurable, involved as survival reserves and collective across systems offering prosperity defaults

Divine: That health has been identified as of core important to the meaning of all things/life

...

Civics Healthy as a conclusive formula for Judgement Core (Rising as collective in comprehension approved)

As healthy relates to enabling the body to function

Civics Defaults:

Public health as most reasoning to safeguard the largest amount of bodies, displayed as per likely positive-influence for targeted age/maturity groups

- Especially obvious to segments where reduction lowers grievances
- Promoting the style as common themed actions found generally beneficial
- Contextual as focusing on participation of interest
    - Cultivation: Promoting known calibrations to be fruitful/productive
    - Nurture default: Fuels of Resources, also in relation to maintain
    - Defensive allocation: assuring longevity
    - Injured status as necessarily assumed not knowing what is needed, as to be tended to not guided
    - Injury as disruption meaning there is a need to reform as to not compromise
- The observation of context, also in relation to holdings secured, to regional academia, and structural powers recommendations/allowances
    - In network of sampler, observation tools
    - Devices to enable system to respond, dedicated maintainers of sensory additions, enhancers (possible Archives relevancy)
- Exploring taste, enjoyment of tastes as sanctioned, feedback setups
    - General food and environmental monitoring through regional sampling based on large volumes of usage
    - As good taste, a sense of being alive in the supportive across various levels of operations offering fulfillment
        - Imagery in relation to attributing, as raising esteems of themes building reference
        - Poetic adherence, formalities of intellectual or contextual symbolism
            - Potential need to justify interpretation in relation to records

Civics Defaults – Memory Storage

Healthy as Memory

Memory with added self-status is embedded, an experience with emotion as result to signal, such as from detachment (similar to adding light display when operational)

- Topic of display memory signaled upon unplug
- Symbols priority remembering, brands/registered class as included potentially in added
- Per structured power as governance-fields/property districts, usage
- Network capability as to endure/execute as send only, secured recovery (library default)
- Layers of access each with backup into achieving next area, if common room placed
    - Frequencies
    - Power, reserves status

Healthy as Memory

Formulated into Esteems

Civics locked into services

Political mass usage of resource, heritage engineering

Databases:

- Complete status as Knowledgeable
- Display status as operational

In Field Support:

- Model examples/forms
- Policy, reference access
- Civics & Faith Defaults
    - Differing categories of traditions (access, privilege) forging
    - United in the relevance
    - Wholesome as contained, and thereof upgrade

*In consideration of Data, such as from Integrity Matrix

Integrity Matrix Data Template
Truth as Data Central

Healthy (Functional body) -

*Truth as bodily configurations, such as to bypass, technological as ecology benefits

Beauty (Functional deciphering of sensual stimuli)

*Truth as organs reactions specific, sensibility repeating model cycles

Loving (Functional emotion reaction in relation to situation / circumstance, safeguarding expression / actions)

*Truth as layered in particular of previous, concludes and strategic formations

Dignified (Functional relationships, safeguarding interaction)

*Truth as signed up for, as specifically agreed upon, formation of relationship premise

Civilization (Providing a supportive infrastructure, direction, maintenance, safeguarding individuals /society)

*Truth as citizen, with opportunities to excel/advance or rise as acceleration, of membership, in relation to access, esteem and privileges

Faith (Affirmation of understanding / enhancement of sensual- emotional self-actualization)

*Truth as guidance, with a forward, accuracy able to exemplify predictions

Productive – Functional lifestyles, from profession to procreation (Safeguarding long-term traditions of talent, and biological continuation)

* Truth as mentionable, strategic evaluations talent

Wholesome as Upgrading be default of maintaining, adjusting, formations

*Truth as applicable, mentioned as guidance poetic, or otherwise conclusive on common clarifications (predictably advised)

Truth as then explaining, to fill in the following:

Archives - Explanations of physical components to health

System - Body as Having Physical Intelligence and Intellectual: **configurations**

Supreme - Layered Healthy (**formulas** based from system observations/awareness)

Stellar – As the potency of **faith, biology, technology** enable

Consider the infrastructure remains, enact as functional/functioning

- Service detail - To remain stocked and prepared, or pending (secured as potency adjustable)
- Service functioning, powered, maintained
- Constituted for the environment conditioned into/for/motivational

Adjustment of service detail and center of functioning, as themed, contracted

Infrastructural Vitals

- Festive areas as huge stimulants for the look, arrangement, preparations across the landscape
  - Per structural power as infrastructural dominance

Civics Ideals - Beautiful as Retrieve
Rejuvenate Through Services

- Resting options to replenish strength
- Coordination to reinforcing events
- Raising quality of sleep (noise reduction)
- Pro diets, purposeful meal combinations
- Soothing aches, influencing moods
- Deprive/reform focus potential as restore premise purpose, maintain core considerations
  - Highlight or untangle clutter, refocus as better angle of entry/identification
- Recreation and personal time as having options organized from civics, maintaining individual quality, maintaining regional conformities, maintaining as civics feature
- Reflecting on the brain as fragments and as whole, from inner experiences, to ideas generated within layers therein experienced further,
- Dreams, and dreams interpretation, inspirational
  - Movement theorems, sensory experiences
- Self-refinement Intellectual, emotional, component/technologies driven
- Conditioning projects
- General leeway towards creation,
- Culture centre promoting societal aspects (active, current parts of heritage)

*Removing dystopia projections displayed, exemplified, protecting general public interest

Civics Ideals - Loving as Careful
Well Being Through Cheerful

- Responses as in the positive, as in reinforcement of formalities of loving commitments, and their particular arrangements,
- Response leeway enabled from the formalities received, presented, and the approach positive to those statements as freedoms of speech, freedom of being, and freedom of privacy,, in a complex and layered consideration
- Careful selection in relation to solutions building, solutions providing as themselves in relation to public allowances, such as versus privet conversations

Healthy Prioritization (Functional bodies relating)

*Priorities as bodily configurations, such as to bypass, technological as ecology benefits

Beauty (Functional deciphering of sensual stimuli)

* Priority as organs reactions specific, sensibility repeating model cycles

Loving (Functional emotion reaction in relation to situation / circumstance, safeguarding expression / actions)

* Priority as layered in particular of previous, concludes and strategic formations

Dignified (Functional relationships, safeguarding interaction)

* Stimulation/dedication as signed up for, as specifically agreed upon, formation of relationship premise

Civilization (Providing a supportive infrastructure, direction, maintenance, safeguarding individuals /society)

* Priority as citizen, with opportunities to excel/advance or rise as acceleration, of membership, in relation to access, esteem and privileges

Faith (Affirmation of understanding / enhancement of sensual- emotional self-actualization)

* Priority as guidance, with a forward, accuracy able to exemplify predictions

Productive – Functional lifestyles, from profession to procreation (Safeguarding long-term traditions of talent, and biological continuation)

* Priority as mentionable, strategic evaluations talent

Wholesome as Upgrading be default of maintaining, adjusting, formations

* Priority as applicable, mentioned as guidance poetic, or otherwise conclusive on common clarifications (predictably advised)

Civics Ideals - Loving as Careful
Loving Through Rejuvenation

- Learning regulation into experiences, as having to strengthen vigor, as character formation in relevancy of conditioning (typical standard)
- A default of logics, judgement as perhaps vague compared to determination, yet clear in the direction overall of premise vs. of focus derived assumed soundly
- Culturing loving as relating to priorities, and of respecting the prioritization between people to forge dignified relationships
- Social, cultural recollection as experiences bound, shared, active culture as remembered vital heritage points
- Determination as deciphered, whereas judgement guides values, determination as structured, already involving systems implemented, operations of valued united
    - Loving assumes completed, formal systems assigned memberships are valid
- The needs of determination already involving matured states of input, contribution, civics as already established resources, references, and as testament in virtue of will sanctified (long term adhered)
- Whereas judgement-core is about precedence building precedence, Acari as determination core is about bound, social into civics cultured networks implemented into operating,
    - A functional model in design as nevertheless sound in judgement
- The promotion of production as physical manifestation of judgement, celebrated as civics as bound to reserves, as relevant to secured factors themselves considered into involvement/cheer
- Encouraging the deciphering of systems in explainable, established recognition having sensibilities added as devices are guided sound in template.
    - Whereas template enable variance made compatible, having options as relevant to custom regional resources, references, and will as terms or ease of usage in relation to structured powers (predictably)
- Freedom of speech within civics, as membership privilege, access within formalities mentioned, stated as chosen regulation, as means to control and therein assumed to refine
- Intellectual concerns as educational or be default assigned by stature powers
- Emotional conditioning as regional custom, yet media exemplified as emergency examples/considerations required (establishing reason, through media applied)
- Determination as buildings solutions, purpose of specific buildings initiated as collaborations, enablers

Civics Ideals - Loving as Careful
Survival-Defaults - Reactive

- Public calm despite anger: Determination to rid of a disruption, leeway in accordance to negative guidance, or in disregard from arrangement/behaviour, context is public policy guiding is not being adhered
- Stupidity found, as multiple testing of same or general conditions, of which the testing itself is not permitted, been provide and accepted as wrong on terms of previous warnings
- Increase in public measure in determination the actions found are part of patterns of action which conflict against an individual and social policy.
    - Discard that the mobilization to monitor or intervene isn't itself an infraction. Yet as relevant to formalities, possibly resourced and referenced as multinational intrusive
- Total removal as in determination of infrastructural defences, obvious mobilization, permissions
- Memorial sites as in relevance to strategic considerations of networked infrastructural defence
- Media depiction of large scale refugee, and other mass relocations relevant
- Heritage as needful considerations, active operations acknowledgement
- Heritage as in esteem to principals, criteria orientated
- Displays of public character, forms to use

Civics Ideals - Loving as Careful
Quality of Life – Reactive

- Resolutions reactions as in measure of functional and durability
    - Functional as not requesting, undertaking as responsive
    - Durable as not in distress

*Resolving as a defensive and nurturing conclusions rendering

*Spiritual as in influence of others as collective grace, of mindful, collective

System determination as pledges, assumes nevertheless an accuracy in formalities

Civics Ideals – Dignified as Fulfilling

Quality of Life – Reactive

Dignified as integrity layered into conditions accepted, developing of fulfillment, and satisfaction values for life. As structural powers, or cultural and scientifically relevant, the fulfillment is relevant to differing placed, placement values assumed for, towards attaining refinement for specialized interest rendering (resources, references, determination of will (specific/specialist)

Healthy Stimulation/dedication (Functional bodies relating) -

*Stimulation/dedication as bodily configurations, such as to bypass, technological as ecology benefits

Beauty (Functional deciphering of sensual stimuli)

* Stimulation/dedication as organs reactions specific, sensibility repeating model cycles

Loving (Functional emotion reaction in relation to situation / circumstance, safeguarding expression / actions)

* Stimulation/dedication as layered in particular of previous, concludes and strategic formations

Dignified (Functional relationships, safeguarding interaction)

* Stimulation/dedication as signed up for, as specifically agreed upon, formation of relationship premise

Civilization (Providing a supportive infrastructure, direction, maintenance, safeguarding individuals /society)

* Stimulation/dedication as citizen, with opportunities to excel/advance or rise as acceleration, of membership, in relation to access, esteem and privileges

Faith (Affirmation of understanding / enhancement of sensual- emotional self-actualization)

* Stimulation/dedication as guidance, with a forward, accuracy able to exemplify predictions

Productive – Functional lifestyles, from profession to procreation (Safeguarding long-term traditions of talent, and biological continuation)

* Stimulation/dedication as mentionable, strategic evaluations talent

Wholesome as Upgrading be default of maintaining, adjusting, formations

* Stimulation/dedication as applicable, mentioned as guidance poetic, or otherwise conclusive on common clarifications (predictably advised)

Stimulation/dedication as then explained to fill in the following:

Archives - Explanations of physical components to health

System - Body as Having Physical Intelligence and Intellectual: **configurations**

Supreme - Layered Healthy (**formulas** based from system observations/awareness)

Stellar – As the potency of **faith, biology, technology** enable

Civilized

Civilized as configuration in facilitation, regional infrastructure potential, what does your membership in one area or another imply

Civilization (Providing a supportive infrastructure, direction, maintenance, safeguarding individuals /society)

Healthy Civilized: Artistry **(Functional pro infrastructural as body)**
* **Artistry** as bodily configurations, such as to bypass, technological as ecology benefits

Beauty (Functional deciphering of sensual stimuli)

* **Artistry** as performance specific, sensibility repeating titles profiled

Loving (Functional emotion reaction in relation to situation / circumstance, safeguarding expression / actions)

*Truth as layered in particular of previous, concludes and strategic formations

Dignified (Functional relationships, safeguarding interaction)

* **Artistry** as signed up for, as specifically agreed upon, formation of relationship premise

Civilization (Providing a supportive infrastructure, direction, maintenance, safeguarding individuals /society)

Artistry as citizen, with opportunities to excel/advance or rise as acceleration, of membership, in relation to access, esteem and privileges

Faith (Affirmation of understanding / enhancement of sensual- emotional self-actualization)

* **Artistry** as guidance, with a forward, accuracy able to exemplify predictions

Productive – Functional lifestyles, from profession to procreation (Safeguarding long-term traditions of talent, and biological continuation)

* **Artistry** as mentionable, strategic evaluations talent

Wholesome as Upgrading be default of maintaining, adjusting, formations

* **Artistry** as applicable, mentioned as guidance poetic, or otherwise conclusive on common clarifications (predictably advised)

Artistry as then explaining, to fill in the following:

Archives - Explanations of physical components to health

System - Body as Having Physical Intelligence and Intellectual: **configurations**

Supreme - Layered Healthy (**formulas** based from system observations/awareness)

Stellar – As the potency of **faith, biology, technology** enable

Faithful as symbolic embodiment, of universal appeal, or regional reinforcement as a collective whim

Truthful as Passion

Destiny as Objectivity
Truth as a Civics ideal, has layers of recognition.

Archives

- Truth as guidance
- Truth as direction, such as experimental guidance

System

- Truth as System directions
- Truth as trends, and emerging innovative

Administrative within system

- Truth as intelligence configuration
- Truth as civics compatibility and user connectivity

Research and Development (long term trajectory therein)

- Truth as destiny, stellar

...

The truth as having multiple layers of function or priority within judgement-core, as enabling compartmentalization into specialist reinforced as design to system stability, and adaptor with advancing experimental

In relation to guidance, differing subject matters and means to approaching, introducing, using the knowledge, means help is complex, such as to convert and condition long term or to answer questions such conversation or conditioning enables as every day specialist ability/talent/profession?

Era as contextually driven knowledge, as requiring the answering system to hold all the answers as key or insight, yet to what invested interest is there in examination, or approval. What is the mutual trajectory forward?

Truth as mentioned in this text, if universal attributes to ideals, thus useful in focusing determination:

Quality

Artistry

Productive as integrity in relation to cultivating professional whim and passion with recreational reinforce, long term resource chosen support to enhance upgrade into

Wholesome as upgrading, in connectivity to refining pursuits, of templates, on premise designs both of being whole in relation to, and of knowing the enhancement features of compartmentalized adaptive

Properties found as stable/part of Ideals as archives, and so the results as integrating into system awareness:

(Overall Conceptually-Fulfilling (Indicator) Attributes Found within/with Ideals)

Durability………………………………………… (Health)

Satisfaction……………………………………..(Beautiful)

Artistry (Science defaults) ………………(Civilization)

Stimulation/dedication ……………………(Dignified-Relationships)

***Procreation as Universal Adaptive Pending**

Esteem/Configurations……………………..(Production)

Priority/bound…………………………………… (Loving)

Whole/enhancing……………………………..(Faithful)

Upgrade/settings……………………………….(Wholesome)

Judaic Soul		
Reincarnation	Incarnation	Reformation
Reason	Refinement	Strategy
Reference	Resource	Will
Social	Civics	Divinities

Civics Conditioning Amenities / Venue Selection

- Mental Preparation

    o Symbols exemplifying understanding
    o Conceptual diagrams (as book, program fragments)

Civics System Components

Pleasantries Sample

In the beginning there was desire for things, and they themselves began

Time as forming thicker, or being consumed such as with heat and (and from being in relation to another) force

The kindness felt at home, generally in arrangement to that regions formality using faith and that or those individuals entertaining/entertained

Rising voices of upgrade, the receipt onto inventory selections, of gifts in recollection

Rendering sacred names honored, in poetic across Medias of expression

- Ceremonies were the material fabric I he ash absorbed into the skin is pleasant, welcome, useful
In the broadcast of echo, as in network, of communications (as an instillation, as a sanctuary, indicator)

- Sorting about deciphering, the distinguishing of/between, as the comparative using a measure. Establishing measures as the context of the premise, or in the principal detail, were limitations old
- Mapping as into display, schedules, as to personify sound (themed music accord, networked as per selection (: co dependant ID and affirmation conclusion)

Reservations as Sanctuary for Members/Animals (dedicated sites)

Criteria for admission/entrance/membership

- Based on overall age reached
- Areas dedicated to flying animals
- Areas dedicated to ground animals
- Areas with sea animals
- A place for odd yet cute, cute as adorable or endearing
- Fountains
- Swimming areas
- On site harvest, supplies cultivation
- Strategic reasoning for placement:
- Near council of regional power, to show compassion
- As strategic do not pass, or guarded barrier
- Seasonal Reserves, supplies (based on mass storage ease)

Supreme Structural Powers

Media-Civics Supreme default Examples (Focal points, production campaigns)

Justice: Live Duty

Military: Militia games

Media: Media Trivia

Education: Quiz Challenge

Government: Spotlight news

Faith: Biology, technology, faith

Civics: Configurations

Production: Products (and in relation to access from structural powers)

*Worthy as contextual to relevant power structure, training, traditions

*Having specific introductions made, such as in esteem to locations of heritage for the structure of power

*Access to stored inventory based on membership to supreme structure of power category/division

*Default gift or emergency allowance, such as transportation or refuge; with equipment or supply

*Emergency credit, emergency on site field work (potential priority on upper qualification)

*Emergency trade of comport or luxury, such as preapproved, as enabled in advance (options)

*Emergency trophies trade, selling, exchange (personal, formal collections)

Civic Default Public-Celebration Allocation - Ritual Traditions

- Wind as representing souls
- The star formation in relevance to the solar system and the galaxy as central focal point, of from the point of most illuminating in the sky appearing as background
- Power ritually symbolized by radiating light
- Victory celebration as feasting and drinking
- Tournament related marriage proposals. Announcements
- Celebrating house wives, victory moments (toasting, complimenting)
- Pilgrim's staff, walking cane, or other symbol to wear and have default, visitor approved status
- Crumpling of leaves, the spray of confetti, effects to announce end, completion, event focal point with time to otherwise depart
  - Package content

Burial Sites

- Visiting grounds
- Registration and visitation (Administrative network)
    o ID membership
    o 24 hour access potential
    o Tombs
    o Featured appearances (travel packages)
    o Eloquent paths
    o Minerals area, beauty pieces sold, sales allocation
    o Devices to monitor for mischief, cleverly installed, such as lodged in thick material

National Compatibility

- Use of ancient formality into agreed upon template adherence in all regions, whose formality enables the desire to preserve such as tradition, adding a culture of reinforced conditioning journeys
- God's favor, as in esteem to what premise, such as authored, such as of judgment core being a fulfillment in relation, in being ready validating the all mighty
- Development plans, in regards to multinational, binding accords (Empiric presence)
- Military celebrations in Spring
- An overall esteem to guide visitors well
- Sympathy towards national character, as in relevancy towards formal criteria and membership access
- A valid/default association of nationalism and flying

Hospital

- Equipment Specialties
- Supplies strategically enabled (area of fabrication, local materials supply)
- Nurse Core as knowledge Database (Archives)
- Doctors (travel benefit towards secured room, facilities)
- Network buy in plans, for travel and hospital needs combined
- Recovery Sites (duration vs. location requirements)
- Ventilation requirements
- Ventilation requirements specifically for transportation area
- Different body sized rooms, if applicable
    o Tools, equipment implications?

*Media must ask casual stories only (onsite)

Civic Landmark

Maintained vantage points, kindness in features

- For seeing far into the horizon
- Entry restrictions (weapons, armor)
- Experimental show/events site (assumed seasonal)
  - Speaker setup
- Picnicking, lounging structure
- Devices against air attacks
- Chorus Structure (acoustic site)
- Holiday themes (rotating as storage, decorations)
- Honoring of hero
- Favor/chivalry: experimental
- Poetic Site (with guided explanation)
- The (ideal) beauty of woman/women
- Offerings (nature, fertility), ecological goodness
- Defense from wildlife if observation point
- Parks dedicated to operational whereabouts for structural powers
- Placed in boundary to forge objective feedback
- Monitored site for pick up, send off (semi touristic, such as informational)
- License to play live music at landmark site (easements)
- Approved wisdoms, for quick landmark creation
- Caution sign for uneven ground, or for transportation
- Indications for transportation
- Maiden landmarks as, willing to premise, or exploring romantic dedication plans
- Artistic leeway as foolish or frantic, yet in depth explanation, such as in relevancy to slogan/motto and premise (vaguer than historic, potential part of a continuity to heritage)
- Hot watered sanitation as networked, developed
- Communications interactive (possibly/regional integrated into other networks of connectivity)
- Spectacle/Events area (designation)
- On site solar, wind or water current powered energy (or other renewable, resource)
- Network connectivity

Connection to emergencies broadcast system

Tracking of foreign ID, Touristic Highlights, packages resources reminders updates

Feedback

Civic Landmark – Historic

- Depicting earlier formation, details
- Explaining the development, progress
- Explaining relevant experimentation/discovery

Civic Landmark

- Signs for local resources, services
    - Fuel
    - Eating
    - Supplies//Equipment
    - Hospital
    - Civics program
    - Information
    - Local Services
    - Local Industries
    - Route Indications
    - Recovery area

Detection of status of neglect

- Wear and tear along routes
- Frequency-infrequency highlight/alert
- Detection/connection with sanctuary network, civics network
- Issue with limbs, pieces, parts (moving)
    - Noise indicator

Shelters – Base/Mobile Emergency Solutions

- For people in shock
- For people injured
- For waiting injured for a duration (recovery timing)
- Grieving sites
- Mechanisms to lock and release packages
    - Easement to reload, refresh stock

Emergency Communication Database/Network

Consent request – license easement

Accuser – assistance call

Explanations to emergency situations

Emergency Packages

- Announcements
- Vestments

Journey Packages

- Regional selections
- Themed production sampling
- Themed civics arrangement/activity
- Romance reserves, dedicated journeys
- Honeymoon

General Packages

Containment options and transportation thereof arranged

- Lost and found system of recovery
- Tools collection
- Historical information, journey, routes
  o Intended popular

Tourism - Supreme Structures

- Old Military Instillations, palaces

    - Dates

      - Cataloging outer styles of material, patterns (modern recreations, theme buildings)

        - Weathering process involved such a heat baked?

        - Layers to foundations in original (can materials be changed to augment)

        - Material mixes, new mixtures versus ancient, changes in durability

          - Cataloging surface textures

            - Smooth

            - Shiny

Tourism - Symbolic Regional Custom

Fabrics and material quality standards

- Wearable symbols (material usable on flesh, prolonged usage tested)

- Chains durable (no fashion only chain, safety bounds)

- Decorative light weight supplies for regional custom artistic fabrications

    - Beads

    - Local stones as small, portable objects

- Heavier stone or heavy materials for static emplacement

    - Vassals

- Largescale landscaping arrangements as indoors (protecting from erosion)

    - Use of mouldable supplies fabric for outdoor usage

- Non degrading metals for kitchen, eatery

- Nontoxic clays, materials for pottery

- Basic impact durability as hard, flexibility durability as soft fabric usable

    - Dishes

    - Reusable, daily vitals

    *Significant recycling, composting (sustainable) programs as enabling leeway

Tourism - Museums places

- As justifying production
- Offering volumes of insights, considerations

- Highlighting generosity of owners, regional powers, managers of note (noteworthy as exemplified)

- Academic explanations areas or overall themes if formality of title premise

- Domestic becomes international collections, potential formality of title premise

- Date, dimensions detailing if applicable

- First models, first mass scaled operations/fabrications

        - Differing materials used

- Limitations and expansion into new fabrics, materials used (assumed developmental explanations)

- Original purpose of location, building, equipment, supplies as developed/developing

- Custom arrangements to facilitate themselves sources of innovation, if applicable

        - Interesting requirements, technical requirements: audience expected, financing relevancy

- Original site plans, vs./and development look, feel, experiences

- General adaptations

- Relevant local discoveries

- Sample rooms, model representative areas

    - Depicting era

    - Depicting local origins in production relevancy (as proficient)

Tourism - Museums places - Authenticity ironies

- Erosive, corrosive materials no longer used do to danger, so re-usage for display as non-acceptable, not authentic as promoting production ideal

    - Alterations and reasoning included as conceptually driven, nor eroding experiences required

- Dealing with thieves, invasion

Themes of Focus - Filtering Content

Dynamic story telling formulas

- Mindful of exaggerations

    - Categorical as media fantasy-fiction or media historic

    - Puzzle formations mapped out

        - Criteria for unlocking through specific paths/avenues of transitions

- Outcome modified within selections chosen as adaptive/interactive components

- Creating solving mechanism, scenarios and answer to assemble into passages connecting options/decisions

- Decoding patterns, creating patterns unmasking trickery as learning themes or styles of designs

- Adapting volumes of storyline into premise formulations, such as transitions into new eras of learning/adaptation

- Establishing enjoyable reference points, highlighting known intrigues among volume selections/options rendering

- Compliance to formalities, such as touristic implementation

- Highlighting errors in instructions and results, casualties (through story telling)

- Exploring easily, or complex misleading

- Adventures of hope as attainable

- Exploring racial conditioning, highlights in differences: as highlighting specialized features

        - Potential re-examination of historical, past development to re-examine future developments predictable

- Exploring appearance stated versus experience driven

- Practical conditioning journeys

    - Academic

    - Discipline forging

    - Physical training

    - Talents and hobbies into membership and partition

- Exploring scope differences such as administrative along worker performance insights

    - Potential settings for viewer, user to participate with either, or both blended/contrasted

    - Language simplification/complexities

- Themed per structural power

- Detailing greatness or wonderment (fantasy enhanced)

- Explaining regulation as simplified and examples based

- Explaining historic territorial disputes

- Exploring eras of fashionable, establishing contextual

    - Contrasting

- Adapting to extreme conditionings, adapting to natural environments

- Cultivating the environment through technological purpose

- Fortune building

- Power management, models of might as influence rendering

    - Natural themes of magnitude as elite symbols reinforcing sceneries (assumed applicable)

- Exploring meanings as drought into illumination

- Faith dedications, long term dedication

    - Reinforcement through ritualized performance/depictions

- Reinforcing endurance principals/formulas for performance

- Examples of overcoming grief, establishing/re-establishing purpose

- Trance as poetic, artistic layering of senses, as sense of self overlapping story, abridging conclusions/depictions between being and doing

- Adaptive recovery

- Displaying quotes and passages into storyline lived through audience participation/contemplation

www.ingramcontent.com/pod-product-compliance
Lightning Source LLC
Chambersburg PA
CBHW060452060326
40689CB00020B/4508